Data Fluencies

## IN SEARCH OF MEDIA

Clemens Apprich, Timon Beyes, Mercedes Bunz,
and Wendy Hui Kyong Chun, Series Editors

*Action at a Distance*
*Archives*
*Boundary Images*
*Communication*
*Data Fluencies*
*Digital Energetics*
*Digital Theory*
*Machine*
*Markets*
*Media and Management*
*Neural Networks*
*Organize*
*Pattern Discrimination*
*Really Fake*
*Remain*
*Technopharmacology*
*Undoing Networks*
*Vector Media*

# Data Fluencies

**Philippa R. Adams, Roopa Vasudevan,**

**Gillian Russell, Kishonna Gray,**

**Wendy Hui Kyong Chun, and Tara McPherson**

**IN SEARCH OF MEDIA**

University of Minnesota Press
Minneapolis
London

meson press

In Search of Media is a collaboration between the University of Minnesota Press and meson press, an open access publisher, https://meson.press



Published by the University of Minnesota Press, 2026

111 Third Avenue South, Suite 290
Minneapolis, MN 55401–2520
https://www.upress.umn.edu

in collaboration with
meson press
Salzstrasse 1
21335 Lüneburg, Germany
https://meson.press

ISBN 978-1-5179-2269-6 (pb)

A Cataloging-in-Publication record for this book is available from the Library of Congress.



UMP BmB 2026

# Contents

# Series Foreword

Our present, characterized by machine-learning processes, technological infrastructures, and emerging data worlds, urges us to think about how media are shaping the conditions under which we live, socialize, communicate, organize, and learn. Searching for media as preexisting conditions of our everyday lives requires us to question the parameters, the limits, the times, the spaces of media today. How do media form to our current situation? And how does the situation make use of them?

This book series looks at these questions by examining the often hidden "terms of media" under which users operate. Rather than producing a set of explanatory keywords to describe media practices, the aim is to understand the conditions under which media are produced, and the ways in which media impact and change those conditions. Clearly, recent technical developments have led to the idea of an always-available knowledge. At the same time, this has transformed the very nature of knowledge production itself, including the assumption that more data must lead to more knowledge. Beyond the mere accumulation of data and knowledge, disciplines—from sociology to economics, from the arts to the humanities—are increasingly in search of media as a way of adding context and reinvigorating their methods and objects of study.

Exploring the situation of digital media, this series asks: What are the conditions of media knowledge today? To answer this question, each book features interventions by several authors, whose approaches to a concept or term (e.g., archives, communication, networks, patterns, machine, markets, vectors) diverge and converge in surprising ways. By bringing together scholars from different intellectual fields and academic regions, this series aims to advance media theory, provoking new descriptions, prescriptions, and hypotheses—to rethink and reimagine what media can and must do today.

# Acknowledgments

We gathered to write this book in Skwiḵw (Whistler) on the unceded, never surrendered territory of the Lil̓wat7úl (Lil'wat) and Sḵwx̱wú7mesh (Squamish) peoples, a truly outstanding mountain setting in which to step away from our other responsibilities and focus on our writing.

We wrote this book over the course of five days—an undertaking that I think most of us were highly skeptical of up until the very last minute—but Jana Mendelski and the team at Booksprints kept us on track and helped us generate something really special in such a short time.

Key to the success of this venture was our deep foundation with these projects and ideas, through the first two years of the Data Fluencies project, including three in person all-team project meetings, and uncountable hours spent forming and anchoring the project in the first place. Every member of the Data Fluencies project contributed to the ideas in this book and how we think about and apply these concepts. The various projects highlighted in these pages were especially shaped by Ioana Jucan (Data Fluencies Theatre Project), Ines Novačić and the USC student team (Reclaim Project), Samein Shamsher (Night School for Data Fluencies), and Ruth Imarhiagbe (Camp Kiki).

This book would not have been possible without Denise Toor, Lab Manager of the Digital Democracies Institute at Simon Fraser University, and assistant editor of this book series. Denise kept us fed and caffeinated, and physically in the correct places throughout the week of writing, but also kept us on track throughout the Data Fluencies project as a whole.

We would also like to thank Mercedes Bunz and the generous reviewers she found for this book, whose feedback and questions offered insight and opportunities to strengthen and clarify our work.

It has been an incredible privilege and honor to work on the Data Fluencies project as a postdoctoral fellow. In my role as program manager I have been able to participate in many fascinating and incredibly different projects, all with the same overarching goal: to figure out how to live in and make our data-filled world better. I have learned so much in the short time I have been involved.

I am very grateful for the experience of writing this book together with such a generous, thoughtful, and capable group of authors. Writing collaboratively with you all was truly an education as well as such an enjoyable experience. So, thank you all for letting me see into your writing processes.

The Data Fluencies project is generously funded through the Mellon Foundation, without whom many of the projects within this book, and the book itself, would not have been possible.

—Philippa R. Adams

# Introduction

Have you ever picked up your phone to quickly check the time, only to find yourself sucked into a vortex of doom or outrage? Racist memes? Articles on how our bosses and devices are spying on us? Posts—clearly written by bots—spreading conspiracy theories like Pizzagate that never seem to die? Videos of the "real" reason teens are addicted to gaming? Messages you suspect were written by AI warning us that we're being manipulated by AI?

Every day, we are exposed to stories or images about the dangers posed by social media, predatory algorithms, and AI. For so many reasons, the future seems in peril, as the threads weaving diverse cultures into civilly engaged societies continue to fray.

It's not just the future, though, that's at risk—it's also our relationship to historical evidence and our present moment. Our social media feeds and much of the internet are already "deep fake" versions of reality, full of lies or distortions parading as facts. These have become the "ground truth" for predictive and generative large language models (LLMs), as the racist texts produced by ChatGPT-X reveal. These outputs then become ground truth for the next generation of LLMs, threatening "model collapse" (Shumailov et al. 2024) and poisoning future conversations and histories. Machine learning algorithms, as they currently exist, are verified as true only if they repeat the often incomplete and inaccurate information they are fed, within certain standard deviations. Simply put: They are tested on their ability to predict or generate plausible versions of the captured or synthetic past (Chun 2021). This undermines our ability to tell truthful and nuanced stories about our present, past, and future, and it forecloses the possibility of different, more just futures that learn from—rather than repeat—past mistakes and injustices.

So, what if we want systems that aspire to other ways of living than disseminating doom, anger, or anxiety? How might we create just and free multivocal futures by learning from the worlds that have escaped, been discarded, covered over, or ignored—worlds that could have been, might have been, and still are?

To begin, we need to understand that every swipe and click opens us to echoes from these worlds. As Kara Keeling reminds us, the task is to "listen [or sense, in our case], with others, for the poetry, the refrains, and the noise a world is making" (2020, ix). When you doomscroll,[1] your every touch sends signals into the air, messages you hope a nearby cell tower will capture. But your signals aren't just read in by the tower; all phones near you read them, even if they can't decrypt them. These signals bounce off other signals in the atmosphere, making the air we breathe an electromagnetic haze. They then usually become light or electrical pulses that travel underground through cables. Coursing along, they generate electromagnetic interference that affects, and is affected by, the lands through which they travel. They are also repeated constantly in order to reach that remote server feeding your habit. Analyzing your current actions (did you hover or swipe?), the app presents you with a so-called personalized feed. But to do so, the machine learning algorithm compares your reactions to millions of others, sweeping you into maelstroms of correlations. But this isn't the only way you're connected to others. At some point, your content has been cleaned by poorly paid moderators in the Global South. And when you grabbed your phone, you were touched by the many who made this action possible: from the person who assembled it to the trucker who transported it; from the miner who unearthed rare minerals to those who cared for the lands it has traversed.[2]

Each step along the way creates opportunities for sensing just futures, presents, and pasts through surprising solidarities, aspirational re-actions, encounters that counter, and moments for play and co-creation. There is no direct route from your phone to you. Your data spreads along multiple paths—movements that recede as narratives of isolation surge. To hear these echoes of multivocal worlds, we need to move with, through, and against data, rather than imagining that by mastering technical protocols and programs, we can finally build the world we want.

This book offers *data fluencies* as creative and imaginative capacities to both grapple with the complexities of data systems and rewrite the scripts we're given. Combining humanities-based critical thinking and methods, computational data analysis, critical data studies, arts-based research co-creation, media making, and community engagement, data fluencies start by realizing that the world our technologies anticipate is not the only one. We can always ride the currents that change, evolve, slip, and subvert.

Data fluencies move beyond literacy, with its focus on reading and writing well within (and thus implicitly accepting) the boundaries of the given world. For example, data literacy in a world dominated by large language models means learning to write the prompts correctly, so the model gives you the result you want. This is by no means simple: You need to know what phrases evoke the best (meaning here the most factually correct) response. You need to tell it to go "step-by-step" to reduce so-called hallucinations (in plain speak, lies) (Yao et al. 2023). You need to change your language to conform to its demands. In contrast, data fluencies move beyond teaching us how to best "prompt" our data-filled world, toward speaking, articulating, and resisting it.

## Data Fluencies Emerge and Flow

In adopting the term "fluencies," we push back on the pathological assumption that a singular "fluency" is the goal. In the field of speech pathology, "fluency" refers to the level of one's proficiency in a particular language. As it is generally understood, "fluency" refers to continuity, smoothness, rate, and effort in speech production (Lickley 2015). It might also focus on sounds, syllables, words, and phrases when joined together (Castro et al. 2014). As scholars in this field suggest, speaking a language "fluently" is the ultimate goal (Bosker et al. 2019). Tests for linguistic mastery thus test for "fluent" and "fluency," but scholars have also contended that there is no consensus surrounding what is meant by these terms (Lickley 2015). Some even argue that a listener's perception is a much better barometer to ascertain "fluency." By moving from fluency to fluencies, we argue that smoothness and continuity are not always ideal, and there is no single version of fluency. Sometimes smoothness needs to be roughed up; sometimes a fast pace needs to be halted; and sometimes meaning can be produced in more than one way.

Data fluencies flow. They matter, but they also shift, morph, repeat, and change. They are *emergent*: They converge at particular times and in specific places in response to the pressures and possibilities the moment offers. They are not a set of ironclad rules, a code script, or a template to follow.

Writer and activist adrienne maree brown offers emergent strategy as a counter to top-down models of action. Building on the work of activists such as Grace Lee Boggs, the speculative imaginings of novelist Octavia Butler, and many others, brown writes, "Emergence notices that small actions and connections create complex systems, patterns that become ecosystems and societies. Emergence is our inheritance as part of this universe; it is how we change. Emergent strategy is how we intentionally change in ways that grow our capacity to embody the just and liberated worlds we long for" (2017, 3). For brown, emergence has value for its fluidity and adaptability but also its connections to the natural world.

Ruha Benjamin (2022) also points us to emergent properties in her model of viral justice. She urges us to attend to small practices and micro tendencies—not to prioritize the individual but to understand how small actions matter. She moves us away from grand theories of social structure to microvisions of social change.

Such microvisions don't stay fixed in place. They are not meant to be scraped or compiled. They each take their necessary form and also flow together to shape a more just world. Benjamin points us toward viruses but also discusses networks of mutual care that have taken shape in the wake of the Covid-19 pandemic, including the more than six hundred groups knitted together under the Mutual Aid NYC banner. While mutual aid networks are sometimes criticized for their piecemeal approach, they might also be understood as forms of practice for other modes of living, a straining toward the worlds we want to inhabit.

Both brown and Benjamin advise us to start small and local, to situate ourselves, to build communities across difference, and to recognize that we can first make changes to the world from where we stand now. Resonating with emergent strategy and viral justice, data fluencies imagine futures arced toward liberation. They ask us to remain in careful and caring relation with each other, with our data and machines, and with the planet. Two of us (Tara and Roopa) spent many hours over the past two years holding space with students in pro-Palestinian encampments that emerged on college campuses. These encampments articulate one form of data fluencies. The students (and sometimes their faculty) came together across many differences—religious, racial, ethnic, national, economic class, and age—to call for a more just world. Their encampments were physical and fluid, taking shape again and again despite ongoing tides of police brutality and administrative hostility. They prioritized mutual care, knowing that their institutions were not caring for them. Their physical encampments interlaced with digital systems brilliantly displayed their fluency in both social media and encrypted networks. They were wary of corporate digital spaces, but they also used them as they needed. They organized horizontally, standing in solidarity with Palestinians and calling for change. Their movement was viral, spreading across countries and the globe, taking shape a bit differently in each locale, and joining a broad global movement.

But even as data fluencies spread, they do not scale, at least not in the way that businesses and platforms define scaling. In Silicon Valley imaginaries, platforms must pursue exponential growth and economies of scale. Venture capitalists and grant applications seek a templated structure that can be copied and pasted across scenarios and propelled into the future. These models strip away complexity and nuance, context, and lived experience.

Scalability also impacts how we shape languages, another aspect of fluency. Official languages aspire to be heard at multiple scales, from the local to the national—and even the global. This desire to float above specific places marginalizes and strangles other languages and voices. As individual speakers, we rarely inhabit languages at a pure, abstracted level. Lived meaning is instead made through the dialects that we speak, through local inflections of language, and even through slang. Dialects ground themselves locally and don't aspire to exponential growth. They break the dream of perfect scalability by creating gaps that demand focus and attention. They trip you up when you encounter them, making you pause and listen. Data fluencies embrace dialects and local knowledges.

Data fluencies also trouble dreams of scalability by embracing sitting with and in repetition. For Black cultures across the globe, repetition is one of the core characteristics of the performed word. For storytellers, it serves a variety of purposes beyond just setting tones and rhythms. While this aesthetic form of communicating dominates this modality, Reed (2007) also believes that repetition "brings clarity to the moment, confirms understanding, gives emotion to or intensifies the endeavor and transmits a determinate idea or concept" (41). When providing a narrative or telling a story, repetition, rhythmically or systematically, lets the audience pick up on the cue and engage in the repetition with the storyteller. This mnemonic technique then becomes a part of the story, and thus a part of the collective memory (Stevens et al. 2017). Similarly, cultures in the Tlicho lands (a self-governed Indigenous region in Canada's Northwest Territories), engaging in drawings and film about the land, are repetitive but transformative, as community members walk and listen to multiple versions of the same story. This repetition then becomes "arrhythmic," blending rhythm (the words of the story) and arithmetic (the repeating of the story) (Gray forthcoming).

In these storytelling practices, every point of the story is and can be next to any other point. Sometimes there is no linear nature to these timelines. Beginnings and endings are multiple. It all depends on when one comes into the story. Older generations have a longer history; their ending might be a youth's beginning. These temporalities collide in a collage of variability with each other: natural fluencies and fluid solidarities.

## How?

In this book, we relay how we—each in our own way and together as a collective—articulate data fluencies. Each chapter is a starting point, focusing on a distinct term—Surprising Solidarities, Re-Act, Counter, Play, and Co-Create—and each reflects echoes of the others.

Chapter 1 reveals the "Surprising Solidarities" embedded within our seemingly closed, data-filled world, as the doom-scrolling example mentioned earlier reveals. Through discussions of Ioana Jucan's devised performances and Roopa Vasudevan's artwork, we show how visions of our world as hyper-polarized or hyper-individuated erase the commonalities that run through our online experiences. To understand the potential of these commonalities—what we call the gaps that bind—we revisit the histories embedded within network concepts such as homophily, which make echo chambers a goal, not an error. Crucially, this listening for commonalities does not erase differences: I am in solidarity *with* you because I'm *not* you.

Chapter 2 investigates new ways to "Re-Act" by examining three research projects on sentiment analysis systems. These systems are a shaping force behind the decision-making of corporations and governments and are often presented as if they are infallible.

But computer-generated analyses of sentiment, affect, and emotion cannot holistically understand human actions. Commercial techniques sanitize the messiness of feeling for corporations' own extractive goals, erasing experiences of sexism, racism, homophobia, and other oppressive forces. By situating the development of sentiment analysis within a longer history, we begin to discern better ways to "re-act" to our feelings.

Chapter 3 takes up what it means to "Counter" as a way to explore the proliferation of hate, misinformation, and toxic masculinity online. We consider the growth in white supremacist organizations across the last two decades, looking at their on- and offline activities. We also examine the deep interlacing of online platforms with this rise in hate. We ask how we might counter such growth and settle on an approach to countering that runs against more typical inflections of the word. To explain our take on "countering," we turn to the Reclaim Project, a student-led Data Fluencies lab at the University of Southern California that is exploring masculinities.

Chapter 4 addresses "Play" through discussions of Kishonna Gray's Camp Kiki, a series of intersectional youth workshops that used the power of gaming to transform lives. To understand the emancipatory power of play, we draw from Booker T. Washington's and W. E. B. Du Bois's reframing of leisure, and we contrast "play in place" with "play out of place." When we play in place, we rehearse scripts we are already given, knowingly or not. When we play out of place, we play ourselves into new realities and potentials. Chapter 5 is a "[Sandbox]" exploring the possibilities of play through engineering.

Chapter 6 considers how to "Co-Create" research practices, drawing from Gillian Russell's Public Night School and Roopa's Creative Resistance Workshops. We show how data-fluent approaches work *with*—instead of just taking *from*—people. By centering rights to research and design, co-creation makes space for the lived experiences and contributions to knowledge made by communities. These projects provide those outside formal academic circles with critical and creative tools for developing collective data fluencies through iterative processes.

We conclude by briefly exploring the wide-ranging and diverse work that is being undertaken by the artists, activists, technologists, and scholars in the broader Data Fluencies network. Together, the projects offer vibrant ways of thinking about, being with, countering, and diverting the streams of data that surround us. We offer these ideas not as an ending point but as an invitation into data fluencies—extended to those who see potential and possibility, even in spaces that seem to be closed from view.

Finally, the coda offers a Data Fluencies Praxis, challenging readers to take up data fluencies within their own lives, interjecting into the norms of engaging and working with data in the pursuit of enabling multivocal data fluencies.

Taken together, the approaches outlined in these chapters help us listen for the worlds that could have been, might have been, and still are. These are starting points for devising more ways to think, act, and imagine—to influence and reshape the currents that flow through our data-driven world.

These starting points are multiple and contrast. In collaboratively writing this book, the six authors all collided at different points during the ideation and writing process. The vastness of thought exercises, along with the experiences of living in each other's words, offered disfluency to a traditionally linear activity. The scripted and unscripted loops that presented themselves in the writing process offered new ways of creating networked—both digital and physical—experiences. We have spent an abundance of time interjecting, pausing, and revising because the traditional approach to engage has not been fluent for us. Data fluencies are, in fact, an interjection into norms around engaging with data work.

Data fluencies thus also seek to reshape how we disseminate our research outcomes and how we do research. Although we are in dialogue with critical data studies, a field that interrogates the social consequences of data and calls for "a comprehensive critique of new regimes of data," we also realize that for our research to matter, we need learn different fluencies (Albrecht and Chun 2024; Dalton and Thatcher 2014). Research, even performed with the best intentions, can create barriers rather than flows, as some of us remembered from a story from our research methods class about quantitative scholars doing research in an underresourced Black neighborhood in Chicago. When they presented their results, they found that their research participants couldn't understand any of the findings because of how research is traditionally presented—with charts, graphs, and other infographic data (Olman 2022). They put this data into words to try to alleviate the problem but quickly realized that even in this supposedly simplified version, the two groups (researchers and community) spoke differently. No matter how they presented the data, the community would not be able to understand the findings—or the subsequent policies that would likely be created based on this data. This is an example of a research failure. There was no ethic of care (Held 2006) in place at any point in the process that considered how the community fit within the research project. The community was an afterthought, used for the benefit of the scholars. As chapter 6 illustrates, a data-fluent approach to research, by contrast, is always intentional in thinking about how we interact with communities: making research protocols accessible; including the community from the beginning of all design phases; and ensuring that there are ways to communicate all research back to the community in ways that are empowering. This is a core tenet of our research ethic.

## Who Are "We"?

This book is shaped by a global field of artists, activists, community members, technologists, and academics who have come together to develop data fluencies. Although it is written by a group of six researchers and practitioners from the broader project—based in North America, out of Vancouver, Los Angeles, Lexington,

Ann Arbor, and Amherst—this book reflects and engages the work of the many folks who are part of the Mellon Foundation–funded Data Fluencies project.

This project as a whole brings together groups that have been working largely in parallel, nonintersecting tracks: social-justice-oriented researchers in the arts, humanities, and data sciences; Indigenous media studies researchers; and intersectional technology developers. It combines qualitative and quantitative methods in ways that do not mimic the user-based surveillance that grounds data analytics. The Data Fluencies project creates sociotechnical systems driven by the needs and imaginaries of impacted communities. It also changes how and what we teach—and who counts as a researcher and teacher.

The "who" expands beyond the members of the Data Fluencies network. We have been inspired by scholar-activists, artist-researchers, theorists, influencers, and community partners, some of whom we have been able to reference in these pages.

Most importantly, we hope that this "who" will include you. Maybe you are a student trying to imagine your future while dealing with the many crises in your present. Maybe you are a teacher—middle school, high school, university—trying to reengage your students in their learning and away from AI-generated assignment responses. Maybe you are an activist, looking for inspiration of how to counter injustice or overreaches of power. Maybe you are an artist, worried about AI extracting training data from your work without your consent, but still wanting to bring joy and multivocality into your efforts. We hope this book will help us move together toward just and free multivocal futures.

## Notes

1 Doomscrolling is defined as the act of compulsively checking the internet, anticipating that you will encounter bad news (Jennings 2020).

2 For more on this, see Crawford (2021); and Bender et al. (2021).

# References

Albrecht, Carina, and Wendy Hui Kyong Chun. 2024. "The Digital Market of Interests and Feelings." In *Politics of Curiosity,* ed. Yves Citton and Enrico Campo. Routledge.

Bender, Emily M., Timnit Gebru, Angelina McMillan-Major, and Shmargaret Shmitchell. 2021. "On the Dangers of Stochastic Parrots: Can Language Models Be Too Big?" *Proceedings of the 2021 ACM Conference on Fairness, Accountability, and Transparency.* 610–23.

Benjamin, Ruha. 2022. *Viral Justice: How We Grow the World We Want.* Princeton University Press.

Bosker, Hans Rutger, Hugo Quené, Ted Sanders, Nivja H. de Jong. 2014. "The Perception of Fluency in Native and Nonnative Speech." *Language Learning: A Journal of Research in Language Studies* 64 (3): 579–614.

brown, adrienne maree. 2017. *Emergent Strategy: Shaping Change, Changing Worlds.* AK Press.

Castro, Blenda Stephanie Alves E., Vanessa de Oliveira Martins-Reis, Ana Catarina Baptista, and Letícia Correa Celeste. 2014. "Fluency Profile: Comparison Between Brazilian and European Portuguese Speakers." *CoDAS* 26 (6): 444–46. Sociedade Brasileira de Fonoaudiologia.

Chun, Wendy Hui Kyong. 2021. *Discriminating Data: Correlation, Neighborhoods, and the New Politics of Recognition.* MIT Press.

Crawford, Kate. 2021. *The Atlas of AI.* Yale University Press.

Dalton, Craig, and Jim Thatcher. 2014. "What Does a Critical Data Studies Look like, and Why Do We Care?" *Society + Space.* https://www.societyandspace.org/articles/what-does-a-critical-data-studies-look-like-and-why-do-we-care.

Gray, Kishonna L. Forthcoming. *Black Game Studies: A Primer.* NYU Press.

Held, Virginia. 2006. *The Ethics of Care: Personal, Political, Global.* Oxford University Press.

Jennings, Rebecca. 2020. "Doomscrolling, Explained." *Vox,* November 3. https://www.vox.com/the-goods/21547961/doomscrolling-meaning-definition-what-is-meme.

Keeling, Kara. 2020. *Queer Times, Black Futures.* New York University Press.

Lickley, Robin J. 2015. "Fluency and Disfluency." In *The Handbook of Speech Production,* edited by M. A. Redford. Wiley-Blackwell.

Olman, Lynda C. 2022. "Decolonizing the Color-Line: A Topological Analysis of WEB Du Bois's Infographics for the 1900 Paris Exposition." *Journal of Business and Technical Communication* 36 (2): 127–64.

Reed, Caroliese Frink. 2007, September/October. "Our Legacy, Our Lineage, Our Love." *Storytelling Magazine* 19 (5): 40–42.

Shumailov, Ilia, Zakar Shumaylov, Yiren Zhao, Nicolas Papernot, Ross Anderson, and Yarin Gal. 2024. "AI Models Collapse When Trained on Recursively Generated Data." *Nature* 631:755–59. https://doi.org/10.1038/s41586-024-07566-y.

Stevens, Garth, Shahnaaz Suffla, Daniel J. Christie, and Mohamed Seedat. 2017. "Critical Psychosocial Mnemonics as a Decolonising Participatory Method: Towards Reclaiming and Refiguring the Archive Through Memory, Stories and Narratives."

In *Emancipatory and Participatory Methodologies in Peace, Critical, and Community Psychology,* edited by Mohamed Seedat, Shahnaaz Suffla, and Daniel J. Christie. Springer International Publishing.

Yao, Jia-Yu, Kun-Peng, Ning, Zhen-Hui, Liu, Mu-Nan, Ning, and Yuan, Li. 2023. "LLM Lies: Hallucinations Are Not Bugs, but Features as Adversarial Examples." https://doi.org/10.48550/arxiv.2310.01469.

[ 1 ]

# Surprising Solidarities

Have you ever received a recommendation or a feed that made you pause? A "wow, that's weird" moment—either because it so got you or because it so didn't? A moment that made you wonder: What does this algorithm know?

You might think that your social media feed—your videos, your posts—are just for you . . . And maybe your friends? Maybe you all subscribe to the same Twitch channels, read the same subreddits, follow the same 'grammers, get the same headlines. Maybe you all get similar recommendations and go down similar rabbit holes.

This is why you're told that you, and everyone else, live in echo chambers. You're sealed in a world that you can't get out of, because you're trapped by the choices you—and others like you or who like you—have made. Sometimes this is explicit: You're told that people who bought X also bought Y. Sometimes it's not.

Why is this happening?

First, recommendation engines and social media presume homophily—the notion that similarity breeds connection, that birds of a feather flock together (McPherson et al. 2001). Because of this, we're clustered according to algorithmically perceived sameness. Because you are friends, you're tied together; because you like the same slightly quirky thing, you're clustered into the same network neighborhood. The same data stream.

**Second, correlation—a relentless mapping of how things correspond—drives these systems. By analyzing Facebook likes, researchers have shown that extroverts like Facebook groups on cheerleading; people who are shy and reserved like fanfiction.net. Gay men like MAC cosmetics; straight men like Sportsnation and Wu-Tang Clan (Kosinski et al. 2013). These correlations divide and seek to hold us in these chambers. They consider not just what most people within a category have liked but also what others—defined in advance as their polar opposite (extrovert/introvert; gay/straight)—have not liked. It's not that the majority of gay men like MAC, but that the majority of straight men don't.**

**So, how do we get out of here?**

Well, what if we literally played with *how* we're played?

Ioana Jucan's *Left and Right, or Being Who/Where You Are* does just that. A devised interactive performance, it probes the affective impacts of online partisan polarization. Taking place entirely online, the performance features both human actors and bots who speak to each other and the audience. The performance reveals that partisan political identity develops from interactions with other people and technologies. It is actively performed by its adherents. It is not fixed or static—it has the capacity to shift, change, and intensify over time.

There are two bot characters: Nick, a "progressive activist," and Kimberly, a "devoted conservative." These personae were adapted from the "Hidden Tribes" project developed by the US organization More in Common. The bots were featured in three main ways: in scripted segments partly generated from the responses given to the actors in rehearsals; in an interlude in which the bots "conversed" with each other, generating responses to each other in real time; and in an interactive piece, in which audience members could type in questions or statements to Nick or Kimberly, who would generate text in return.

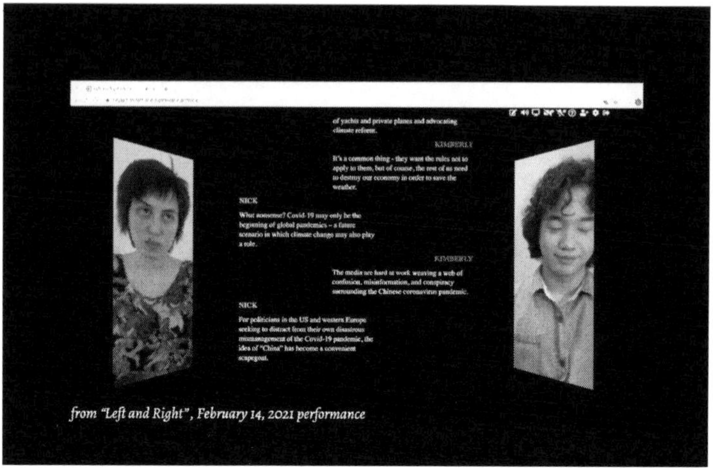


[Figure 1.1]. A screenshot of the Left and Right performance from February 14, 2021. Courtesy Ioana Jucan.

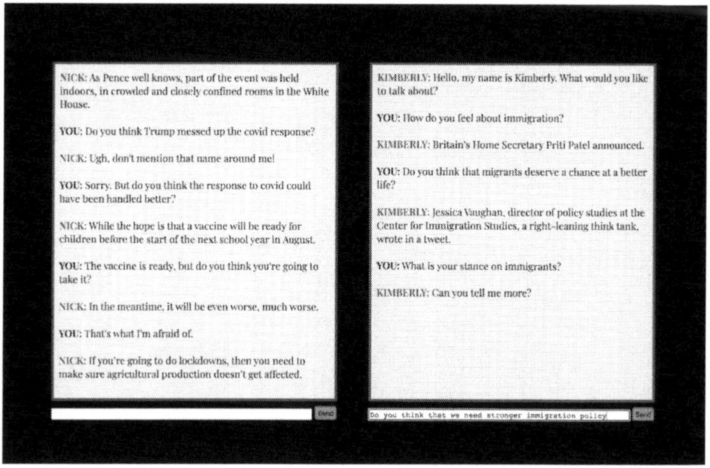


[Figure 1.2]. A screenshot of audience interactions with bots Nick and Kimberly. Courtesy Ioana Jucan.

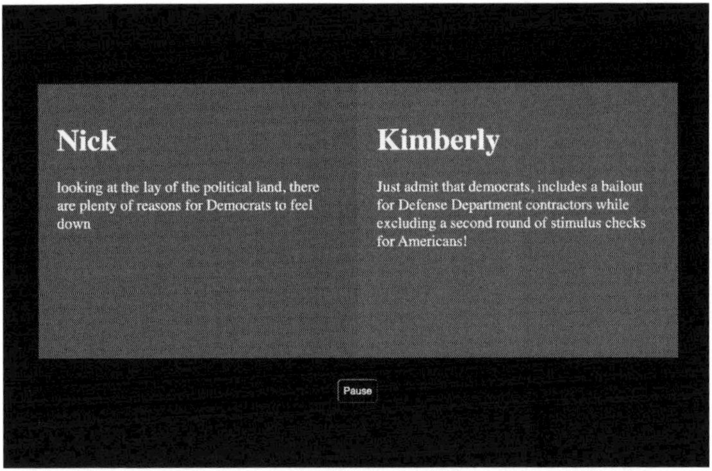


[Figure 1.3]. A screenshot of the conversation between bots Nick and Kimberly. Courtesy Ioana Jucan.

The team trained the bots using news articles from MediaCloud, a media-tracking database that enables users to aggregate articles sourced from various outlets and place them into bins. Initially, the team fed each bot one thousand articles from bins associated with Twitter users who fit Nick and Kimberly's personae. The team thought that by training the bots on large volumes of this partisan content, they would be able to construct responses to a variety of situations that made sense for each character (Jucan et al. 2021).

But instead of strengthening a partisan perspective, training the bots on so many stories produced banalities. The team found that even with one thousand articles each—a fraction of the content available in the MediaCloud bins—the bots "were not speaking in the polarized language we wanted them to" (Jucan et al. 2021). On the contrary, Nick and Kimberly produced random utterances and statements that were matter-of-fact in tone, and they often simply didn't make any sense at all. The team tried adding more articles, but found that the more they included, the weaker the partisan language became.

To solve this problem, the team shifted gears and retrained the bots using a curatorial approach. They reduced the amount of content the bots were fed and instead hand-selected fifty articles per bot, which they thought best reflected the typical news diet of each character. Only then could the bots be perceived as coherently "Left" or "Right." The polarized identities could not simply be reverse engineered into the bots just by dumping lots of news articles into them; instead, it took careful crafting and selection to arrive at any kind of convincing dialogue (Jucan et al. 2021).

This is a remarkable insight, which reveals how much must be erased for us to see and construct polarization. So, what happens when we sit with this surprising algorithmic revelation of how much we have in common? What might this solidarity—this unexpected echoing of divergent voices—tell us about the limits of algorithmically engineered echo chambers? Correlations not only divide, but they also create fluid connections that overwhelm seemingly neat clusters.

## Solidarities, Online

As we pointed out in the introduction, users are never alone, even when they think they are. What you see depends not only on your clicks but on how your clicks and hovers correlate with others, in an algorithmic imaginary constructed solely through homophily, sameness that binds. If everything you see and do echoes with the actions and perceptions of someone else, which resonates in turn with someone else still, a chain of actions would seem to join us together.

We could imagine these constant correlations as forms of solidarity—except that solidarity implies people intentionally united together, five fingers clenched together in a fist or supportive networks of mutual care. Instead of deliberate community, algorithmically constructed correlations are pitched as "hidden tribes."[1] But again, "finding" your tribe entails training out most of what brings people together. To create ties that bind, all that touches us in common needs to be hollowed out. The only things solid in a network are the gaps, which touch multiple ties at once (Chun 2021a).

But crucially, correlations don't simply confine users to a network neighborhood. Large language models (LLMs) scrape the entire internet and build a map of invisible textual clusters that escape human comprehension. They then give you one answer, covering over this morass. But these incomprehensible links, born of theft and capture, can also create more *solid* solidarities, and ways of saying "I'm with you" in the world of data analytics.

For example, in response to the rise of image generators like DALL-E and Midjourney, artists Holly Herndon, Molly Crabapple, and Kelly McKernan have led several efforts calling on their peers to fight against the current, collectively protest, opt out, or otherwise refuse the voracious capture of their work within these systems. These generative models are developed using vast quantities of work that artists have posted online for various purposes. None of these include being harvested by a tech company to train their proprietary AI systems—with no credit or compensation for their contributions—to fuel corporate profit. Herndon, along with collaborators Mat Dryhurst, Patrick Hoepner, and Jordan Meyer (collectively known as Spawning.ai), developed and launched the site *Have I Been Trained,* which allows artists to search for their work in popular AI training datasets and request that it be removed by adding it to a "Do Not Train" registry (Edwards 2022). Over 1.4 billion such requests were made in under a year from the site's launch (Chow 2023a). In 2023, in collaboration with the Center for Artistic Inquiry, Crabapple drafted an open letter urging news organizations to refrain from using AI-generated illustrations and graphics, which to date has amassed over one thousand signatories (Lawson-Tancred 2023). Alongside two other artists who had also seen their work appropriated and replicated by AI systems, McKernan sued Stability AI and Midjourney in 2023, joining lawsuits by Getty Images and the *New York Times,* which all argue that the rampant use of online content to train these models amounts to little more than direct theft (Noveck 2023; Chow 2023b).

These artists are banding together—regardless of differences in medium, career stage, or level of renown—to push back against what they see as a common issue: the exploitation of their work by powerful companies with no regard or respect for the labor that went into making it.

What's crucial about this form of solidarity—and indeed solidarity more generally—is that it implies and respects differences. I am in solidarity with you. I am not you. *I am in solidarity with you because I'm not you.* These practices also underpin many forms of progressive activism and mutual care, creating vibrant networks of commonality in and through difference, flowing together as needed. Again, what is solid on a network graph is not a tie or connection but the gaps that touch. Gaps that are never empty but rather filled with all that we hold and experience in common.

If this is so, how might we begin with these whited-out commonalities and engage multivocal data fluencies?

## Doubling Data, Together

*dataDouble*[2] by one of us (Roopa) does just that.

A digital portraiture project begun in 2018, *dataDouble* is a web browser extension, available for download on Google Chrome and Mozilla Firefox. Upon installing the extension, you are prompted to upload a photo of yourself; the extension then runs in the background for the next fourteen days, tracking your browsing behavior. Afterward, you can download a portrait. This image is the same photo that you initially uploaded to the extension, but with a twist: It has been computationally edited and manipulated by the amount and types of browsing you've done. A combination of up to six digital effects—posterization,[3] edge detection, noise, saturation, contrast, and gamma[4]—are applied to the image, based

[Figure 1.4]. A screenshot of the *dataDouble* Chrome extension and the resultant portrait of the artist. Courtesy Roopa Vasudevan.

on metrics such as the number of different news sites you visited, your shopping or banking, or your use of search engines.

The first time the project was run, fifteen volunteer participants used the browser extension for two weeks and then sent their final portraits to Roopa. In follow-up interviews, Roopa guided the participants through the project "code book," which outlined the rationale for applying specific effects based on related browsing behavior. These discussions also touched on broader questions of surveillance and identity, as well as how the participants felt about the constant tracking and targeting that they encounter online.

According to Roopa, participants would attempt to rationalize their portrait's appearance. Surprised that their portrait didn't look how they expected it to, the participants reached for excuses to explain why their "data double" was a poor reflection of who they imagined themselves to be online. They would justify certain effects by claiming that they were related to specific, unusual life circumstances;

[Figure 1.5]. *dataDouble* installed at the National Liberty Museum (Philadelphia), June 2023. Courtesy Roopa Vasudevan.

for example, shopping online for a new fridge because their old one broke, or spending more time on social media than normal because they were looking for a job.

When all the participant portraits are viewed together, it is striking to see how similar they appear from far away. At first glance, you wouldn't imagine that anything different happened to generate each of these portraits: They all contain noise; they all have their edges articulated in some way; they all are rendered in fewer colors than a regular photo would use. It is only when you inspect each more closely that you start to see the differences. One image might be slightly more saturated than another, a reflection of a greater diversity of news sources. One might contain more contrast, a result of higher search engine activity. And one might be covered with so much noise as to seem almost pixelated, reflecting many visits to niche or uncommon websites.

This oscillating similarity and difference of the portraits encapsulates the contradictory effects of large-scale data analytics on our identities and self-perceptions. What is, on the surface, a hyper-individualized interpretation of a single person's behavior is created by making you into one of many. The algorithm might know you, but it is only because it thinks it knows a bunch of other people like you.

While often surprising, seeing how their browsing affected their portraits concretized for the participants the way their data was being mined. It made them understand that if this was happening to them, it was also happening to others. The project made them aware of the larger injustices of dataveillance.[5] As one participant articulated in their interview, "This is making me think about how my identity can be, sort of, instrumentalized in weird ways. Through similarities with others . . . because it's part of a group, those similarities will be what can be instrumentalized" (Vasudevan 2021, 18). In the face of being sorted, grouped, and categorized in the name of individualization, solidarity can emerge when we recognize that what's happening with "me" is also happening to others, even if it might take on a different form.[6]

## Intending Solidarities

By revealing similarities across seemingly hyper-individualized processes, *dataDouble* raises the possibility of creating more fluid solidarities. Fluid, not because they are less strong or trustworthy but rather because they are born of and thrive through movement, even turbulence.

Fluid solidarities are eddies—whirlpools that create countercurrents and spaces for stasis. They may be short-lived, emerging and dispersing, but they are nonetheless powerful. They show us other ways to congregate, other ways to be.

Online, our data is always in motion, and it is because we move that we can be "captured" by these systems that relentlessly

[Figure 1.6]. The Corryvreckan Whirlpool (United Kingdom). Photograph by Walter Baxter.

map our constant changes of state (Agre 1994; Chun 2016). Fluid solidarities engage the algorithmic and the human—and their intermingling—to merge across multiple differences.

Fluid solidarities, though, are important but not enough. There is nothing that guarantees in advance that these will be progressive or just. Indeed, we might consider the manosphere, with its entangling of "men going their own way," "incels," and "dark enlightenment," as a form of fluid solidarity, constantly morphing and updating its trolling and threats to evade detection.

Fluid solidarities—if they are to aspire to just worlds—must engage with the histories and communities whited out in these so-called gaps. The history of homophily starts us on this path. As one of us (Wendy) has shown elsewhere, the concept of homophily emerged from studies of US residential segregation, in particular the intimate friendship formation patterns of white liberals and illiberals living in a biracial housing project (Lazarsfeld and Merton

1954; Chun 2021b). What this means—given that homophily grounds social networks and recommendation systems—is that echo chambers aren't an unfortunate mistake; they're a goal.

Echo chambers, though, only exist by erasure—by creating gaps. To show how homophily develops through "common values," the researchers ignored most of their data: All the responses of Black residents, who comprised half the population (because they did not have enough illiberal or ambivalent friends to count), and the white ambivalents, who comprised the largest category. They also ignored all the ties that couldn't be captured by close friendships—connections that they promised to document in a report that remains forever forthcoming.

In the archive, we find echoes of these myriad "other" friendships and commitments to living together that homophily dampens. We also find common cares and concerns that cut across the residents, whose responses the researchers almost always divided by race. Even in the "officially sanctioned interviews," there was palpable resentment against the management, who oversaw the residents in so many ways. By focusing solely on homophilic relations, we miss these common concerns and cares.

This chapter reveals that by inhabiting the structures usually used to dampen our echoing connections—such as homophily and correlations—we find surprising solidarities. Correlations do not simply divide; they also reveal commonalities, which are often regarded as errors and deleted, or dismissed as unimportant. As the history of homophily shows us, to ensure that questions of social justice remain in focus as we create fluid solidarities, we need to listen for the echoing relations whited out by seemingly technical defaults. Crucially, data fluencies do not demand that we be identical but instead perform solidarity across difference—a topic addressed in the next chapter.

## Notes

1 As Jodi Byrd has pointed out, the terms "tribe" and "digital natives" repeat a pattern of appropriation that both covers over colonization and claims the status of the "real victims/heroes." As they also presciently note: This abjection of "colonialism, genocide, and tribalism," which seeks to create "like-minded tribes," constantly produces "Indians so that the United States and the banks can play cowboy" (Byrd 2014, 59).

2 This project takes its name from a prevalent concept in surveillance studies, first articulated by Haggerty and Ericson (2000) as an abstract representation of a human counterpart, which takes on its own life as it is disassembled and reassembled in myriad configurations in order to fit specific needs or functions. The artwork uses the "data double" concept—as applied to the human face—to explore themes of surveillance, identity, and algorithmic sorting and categorization.

3 Posterization is the reduction of the number of hues used in rendering an image.

4 The gamma values are responsible for adjusting the luminance of an image; in other words, they make the lights lighter and the darks darker.

5 As outlined by Raley (2013, 214), dataveillance is the "disciplinary and control practice of monitoring, aggregating, and sorting data."

6 The *dataDouble* project is in ongoing development with plans for a mobile version, since participants have noted that they use their phone and computers differently. Based on a workshop run in 2023 with Ganaele Langlois, Alex Juhasz, and Ioana Jucan, Roopa will develop more opportunities for people to come together to think and speak in solidarity about the effects of correlation and surveillance on their online practices, shifting from one-on-one interviews to group conversations.

## References

Agre, Philip E. 1994. "Surveillance and Capture: Two Models of Privacy." *The Information Society* 10 (2): 101–27. https://doi.org/10.1080/01972243.1994.9960162.

Byrd, Jodi. 2014. "Tribal 2.0: Digital Natives, Political Players, and the Power of Stories." *Studies in American Indian Literature* 26 (2): 55–64. https://doi.org/10.5250/studamerindilite.26.2.0055.

Chow, Andrew R. 2023a. "Time100 AI: Holly Herndon." *Time,* September 7. Retrieved from https://time.com/collection/time100-ai/6309468/holly-herndon/.

Chow, Andrew R. 2023b. "Time100 AI: Kelly McKernan." *Time,* September 7. Retrieved from https://time.com/collection/time100-ai/6309445/kelly-mckernan/.

Chun, Wendy Hui Kyong. 2016. *Updating to Remain the Same: Habitual New Media.* MIT Press, 2017.

Chun, Wendy Hui Kyong. 2021a. "The Space Between Us: Network Gaps, Racism, and the Possibilities of Living in/Difference." *Catalyst* 7 (2). https://doi.org/10.28968/cftt.v7i2.34903.

Chun, Wendy Hui Kyong. 2021b. *Discriminating Data: Correlation, Neighborhoods, and the New Politics of Recognition.* MIT Press.

Edwards, Benj. 2022. "Have AI Image Generators Assimilated Your Art? New Tool Lets You Check." *Ars Technica,* September 15. Retrieved from https://arstechnica.com/information-technology/2022/09/have-ai-image-generators-assimilated-your-art-new-tool-lets-you-check/.

Haggerty, Kevin D., and Richard V. Ericson. 2000. "The Surveillant Assemblage." *The British Journal of Sociology* 51:605–22. https://doi.org/10.1080/00071310020015280.

Have I Been Trained? n.d. "About." Retrieved from https://haveibeentrained.com/about.

Jucan, Ioana B., Roopa Vasudevan, Anthony G. Burton, Tong Wu, and Yuguang (YG) Zhang. 2021. "Performing 'Left and Right.'" *Theatre Journal* 73 (3): E-9–E-14. https://doi.org/10.1353/tj.2021.0064.

Kosinski, Michal, David Stillwell, and Thore Graepel. 2013. "Private Traits and Attributes Are Predictable from Digital Records of Human Behavior." *Proceedings of the National Academy of Sciences* 110 (15): 5802–5. http://www.pnas.org/content/110/15/5802.full.pdf.

Lawson-Tancred, Jo. 2023. "Molly Crabapple Has Posted an Open Letter by 1,000 Cultural Luminaries Urging Publishers to Restrict the Use of 'Vampirical' A.I.-Generated Images." *ArtNet News,* May 3. Retrieved from https://news.artnet.com/art-world/open-letter-urges-publishers-not-to-use-ai-generated-illustrations-2294392.

Lazarsfeld, Paul F., and Robert K. Merton. 1954. "Friendship as Social Process: A Substantive and Methodological Analysis." In *Freedom and Control in Modern Society,* edited by Morroe Berger, Theodore Abel, and Charles Page. D. Van Nostrand Co.

McPherson, Miller, Lynn Smith-Lovin, and James M. Cook. 2001. "Birds of a Feather: Homophily in Social Networks." *Annual Review of Sociology* 27:415–44. https://doi.org/10.1146/annurev.soc.27.1.415.

Noveck, Jocelyn. 2023. "Visual Artists Fight Back Against Artificial Intelligence Companies for Repurposing Their Work." *PBS News,* August 31. Retrieved from https://www.pbs.org/newshour/arts/visual-artists-fight-back-against-artificial-intelligence-companies-for-repurposing-their-work.

Raley, Rita. 2013. "Dataveillance and Counterveillance." In *Raw Data Is an Oxymoron,* edited by Lisa Gitelman. MIT Press.

Vasudevan, Roopa. 2021. *dataDouble: A Project by Roopa Vasudevan.* Self-published.

[ 2 ]

# Re-Act

Have you ever wondered why our machines keep asking us how we feel—when they don't seem to care?

Facebook asks us, "What's on our mind?" We like or hate posts; we push green smiley faces or red frowns, but nothing seems to change.

One of us (Tara) works at a large private university in the United States that is intent on taking its employees on a "culture journey" to improve campus morale as a reaction to a series of egregious ethical breaches covered up by senior administration. By deploying polling software and conducting HR-driven "listening sessions," the university repeatedly surveyed the faculty about their feelings over three years. Unsurprisingly, the process doesn't seem to be improving trust in the administration—but it did generate several working groups, lots of word clouds, and numerous reports that seemed ill-suited to address the systemic issues that plague US universities, from spiraling student debt to the casualization of labor. The university endlessly asked the faculty how they felt, all while ruthlessly blocking unionization efforts, student protests, and demands for divestment. Solidarity built from word clouds feels thin indeed.

Many corporations are turning to these kinds of software systems, called "bossware" to better manage and control their employees, all under the guise of caring or of making work "feel" better. Bossware constantly surveils you as you work. It logs your keystrokes, takes screenshots, records mouse movements, activates webcams and microphones, and periodically takes photos of you. But Bossware isn't just about surveillance; it also tries to predict what you could do, so it can react before you act up. Bossware reads everything that you write and then uses sentiment analysis to determine your risk level. Sentiment analysis systems are computational tools that assign scores to chunks of text; at their most simple, they categorize inputs as positive, negative, or neutral. You're flagged as a potential threat when your sentiment score shows you're disgruntled, or if your sentiment score radically changes.

But most of the time, these systems don't even work properly, as one of us (Pippa) demonstrated in her in-depth analysis of VADER, a lexicon-based sentiment analysis system.[1] Pippa analyzed the sentiments present in over ten thousand Twitter posts on the release of the *Captain Marvel* film in 2019—the Marvel Cinematic Universe's first female-led superhero movie in ten years—comparing VADER's results with her own assessment of the same tweets (Adams 2023).

Posts containing excited, gushing, anticipatory fan reactions—or marketing hype—were easy for the machine to label as positive. But it had a hard time tagging sexism as negative. VADER did not classify as negative posts criticizing the lead actress for not smiling enough, pitting superhero women against each other, or suggesting a boycott of the film for not catering to the default white male nerd. Also, the emotionally charged and highly gendered reactions to the film were often too nuanced and too contextual for VADER to correctly classify. For example, the system seemed to struggle with the gendered use of emojis. Many tweets that included the crying face (😂) emoji were categorized by the computer as negative in sentiment, even though the tweet contained expressions suggesting that the emoji was actually signifying "happy tears"—a sign of strong emotions that society often considers to be more feminine in nature.

We shouldn't be surprised. Sentiment, affect, and emotion aren't literal—they are more complex and contextual than computational systems can easily ascertain. Further, when we tweet about a movie or post a selfie, we aren't reacting instinctively—we're re-acting, creating our narratives as fans or microcelebrities. Sentiment analysis systems misrecognize intentional re-actions as literal indications of our subjective state and are then used to make decisions about us.

Why do corporations use sentiment analysis systems when they seem to be constantly failing? Why do they keep tracking our feelings when they seem not to care? How does this drive us to operationalize our feelings and measure our moods, fix us in place—and how might data fluencies offer an opportunity to re-act differently?

## What Was Sentiment Analysis Missing?

Pippa's sentiment*al* attachment to the film, comics, and character led her to dig deeper into the assessments made by VADER in order to uncover what the sentiment analyzer couldn't seem to understand. This required acts of translation, as computational tools have their own languages. In doing this work, Pippa had to learn to express her questions and instructions in a new way of speaking, of interacting with this scale of data to address her research questions. To fluidly translate these research questions into a program like Python to run the sentiment analyzer, she had to acquire the vocabulary, syntax, and semantics—she had to gain new streams of fluencies, in addition to the understandings of sarcasm, memes, and the context of the Marvel Cinematic Universe and comics fans that she brought into this work.

Social media demands its own fluencies as well. The mythos of social media is embedded within its interactivity, its context. And yet this dictionary sentiment analyzer, created for a social media environment, was making errors based on that fluid, contextual, interactivity. The problems VADER had with parsing emoji use, its inability to classify sexism as negative, and questions of what the negativity in these posts was being directed toward, even within the same "topic," compounded in this research to illustrate the instances where computational methods do not have the fluency necessary to make connections—or has not yet been developed with such fluencies in mind. VADER could not understand the language of these posts in this space where contexts converge to increase the difficulty of reducing complex currents of posts into simply positive, negative, or neutral.

And yet, the task of determining sentiment, at scale, is still one that continues.

## Surveilling Employees

The constant probing of "how we feel" is especially creepy at work. Our employers appear to be very interested in asking us "how we are." Pippa and Evan Donahue co-lead a project focused on boss-ware with other researchers at Simon Fraser University's Digital Democracies Institute as part of the Data Fluencies Project. The team's research has shown that, while these tools are marketed as neutral measurement tools (Donahue et al. 2025), they produce very particular and skewed understandings of sentiment—while crucially normalizing surveillance of employees in all areas of their work.

In 2024, this research tried to reproduce the findings featured in a white paper by AwareHQ, which presented results from their proprietary sentiment analysis system. It argued that an endless parade of entitled "Karens"[2]—more than any other structural element of working conditions—was responsible for employee turnover (Aware 2023a). In an ironic twist, corporations justify their use of bossware—and their surveillance of workers—by framing it as protecting and caring for their workers.

AwareHQ reported that they analyzed 152,716 Reddit posts, collected between January and April 2023 from the subreddits for eight major retailers. The Data Fluencies team used Llama-2, VADER, and Detoxify to try to replicate these proprietary results. We reported similar findings in some areas; however, we also found some intriguing differences.

When compared to the rest of the dataset, the number of posts mentioning interactions with "Karens" is far too small to be a central driving force for "no one wanting to work anymore." Much like Jucan's *Left and Right* performance discussed in chapter 1, AwareHQ had to massage their data to produce the polarization everyone anticipates. This Karen-blaming recalls the *Captain Marvel* example discussed earlier but with a twist. Many of the tweets that Pippa hand-coded as negative because they contained markers of sexism or misogyny, VADER categorized as positive (Adams 2023, 150). AwareHQ recognized Karens as tied to negative emotions, not because they were sexist posts but rather *because* of sexism.

Crucially, although the analysis confirms that "coworker" is more consistently toxic than "supervisor," "boss," or "CEO," "team"—a term that AwareHQ did not include in its public materials—appears seventeen times more frequently than "coworker," and is more "healthy" than all other words.

Bossware like AwareHQ thus divides workers and customers from each other both within and across groups. This reinforces power asymmetries in favor of corporations, who continue to make record profits while employees face stagnant wages and precarious employment, and customers suffer from increasing prices and automation. At a time when labor movements are again picking up steam in many countries, corporate sentiment analysis performs a sleight-of-hand, directing workers' attention elsewhere to prevent them from reacting in a unified way. But we also must remember that bossware isn't new; in fact, sentiment analysis has always been about surveilling workers. 

## Good Enough to Justify Surveillance; Bad Enough to Justify Greater Surveillance

Why do we think sentiment matters? Where did sentiment analysis come from?

We think that sentiment matters because of a series of highly influential and controversial experiments jointly run by researchers at the Harvard Business School and executives at the Hawthorne Western Electric (WE) factory in Cicero, just outside Chicago, from 1927 to 1932 (Albrecht and Chun 2024). These experiments are considered key to the emergence of corporate Human Relations.

In the most famous experiment, five factory workers—women operators producing relays (electronically operated switches)—were segregated for special study. The researchers placed these women in a special test room, in which everything was measured and controlled, to determine the relationship between productivity and variables including temperature, humidity, hours of sleep, work breaks, free lunches, and reduced hours. They were repeatedly told to work as they usually would, to ignore the observer and all the interested parties—executives, professors, observers—who kept traipsing through their room.

These women were under constant surveillance. They underwent medical examinations every six weeks. They were asked to record what they ate, how many hours they slept, and what their responsibilities were at home. Their conversations were recorded by a male test room observer, also in the room. His job was to keep accurate records of all that happened and to create and maintain a friendly atmosphere in the test room—that is, to ensure that the women cooperated. All these factors were measured against how many relays these women produced when they worked genuinely.

[Figure 2.1]. *Women in the Relay Assembly Test Room,* ca. 1930. Courtesy of AT&T Archives and History Center.

This experiment, originally projected to last for a few months, continued for five years and expanded to include interviews with about twenty thousand individual employees because the initial results were both anticipated and unanticipated. At first, breaks, shorter hours, and free lunches increased productivity. But then, in the three-month period in which all the accrued benefits were taken away, something surprising happened: Productivity remained high. So, something else mattered.

Well, this experiment accidentally changed how these women were paid. Usually, they worked in groups of about one hundred, and their pay would depend on everyone in their group. In the test room of five, they had far more control. But the experimenters thought it had to be more than money—it couldn't be as simple as paying workers more—so they set up two other experiments. They first selected another five women and only changed the pay structure. They found that productivity went up but not as much as the women in the test room. Next, they segregated a group of linemen in a test room. They gave them the same perks and found that extra breaks and so on made no difference. Production was always constant. These men, of course, were deeply suspicious of management.

After conducting other experiments on female and male workers, all of which failed to reproduce this result, the researchers argued that worker sentiment drove productivity. Their "great *éclaircissement*" (Roethlisberger 1941, 15)—their big takeaway—was that "the behavior of workers could not be understood apart from their feelings or sentiments," which were not logical but subjective (19).

Intriguingly, it was the women themselves who provided this answer. In response to the question "What do you think has made it possible for you to increase your earnings since you have been on the test?," they stated: "greater freedom," "the absence of bosses," "more personal attention," "the opportunity to set one's own pace and to earn what one makes without being held back by a big group." According to the researchers, these women were having fun.

Now if these women were having fun, they, as the researchers themselves point out, were having fun and feeling free in the oddest of circumstances. The women were far more thoroughly supervised than they ever had been in the regular department. They were watched by an observer of their own, an interested management, and outside experts. But, they argued, the character and purpose of the supervision were different and were felt to be so. These women knew they were taking part in an important and interesting experiment. They were asked how they were, consulted about every change, and interviewed constantly. They had an audience.

But the researchers' "great enlightenment" almost didn't happen. As Melissa Gregg (2018) and one of us (Wendy) have stressed, the company had first to kick out two of the initial workers, 1a and 2a.

They were replaced because their productivity did not improve with either incentives or threats, and because they ridiculed their peers in Polish for working like fools (four out of the five original operators were Polish American). As the archives reveal, these experiments, like the housing study discussed in chapter 1, were experiments in white Americanization. Cicero was a sundown town—no Black Americans could be there after dark, and the factory did not hire any Black workers until after World War I.

The unrelenting drive for greater productivity in the test room emerged once an Italian American woman became an operator and pushed the rest to work harder. She was the most educated out of the group, the most ambitious, and the main breadwinner of her family. Shortly after the experiment started, her mother died, so she was responsible for maintaining the household, including her father and brothers, in all senses of the word. As she put it, she needed the money.

After the researchers "discovered" the importance of sentiments, they started interviewing all the other workers in the factory. Initially, they extracted keywords from these interviews as positive or negative. They soon realized that this did not capture the breadth of worker sentiment. They transcribed interviews word-by-word and started analyzing them for "hidden," almost psychoanalytic, reasons for discontent, such as problems with authority figures. In other words, the failure of sentiment analysis provoked further, more detailed surveillance.

Crucially, these experiments took place during a time of high labor unrest and unionization. Sentiment analysis thus has a long history of thwarting true cooperation and solidarity, instead trying to get workers to produce beyond their capacity.

What's remarkable about these experiments across a century, from Bossware to Hawthorne, is how much sentiment analysis remains the same! It doesn't work now and didn't work back then. The quantification and reduction of worker interviews into positive or negative did not capture the breadth of worker sentiment. The failure of sentiment analysis drove further surveillance. Sentiment analysis is just good enough to justify surveillance and yet bad enough to justify greater surveillance. 

## Re-Acting to Surveillance

We have to remember, though, that what's read as "genuine" via sentiment analysis is anything but. Think of how Americans and Canadians respond to the question "How are you?" Rather than telling you how they really are, they usually say, "Fine, how are you?" It's an interchange devised to make social interactions easier by asking folks to essentially lie about how they are—or more precisely cover over their feelings. In fact, actually telling someone how they are—something that one of us (Wendy) found that Germans tend to do—undermines social interactions. In response to "How are you?" we become characters—dividing our so-called real self from our social one.

This is clear in the historical record. The Italian American woman in the test room was an operator in all senses of the word, and she and her colleagues knew that their work and responses affected everyone else—their coworkers received breaks because they cooperated with the researchers. They became minor celebrities. They survived five years of intense surveillance by treating their monitors as an audience. They were actors playing a part. As if leaving breadcrumbs for their "bosses," they talked of films and their favorite characters all the time.

These women, and their reactions to their situation, resonate with insights drawn from Pippa's work on fans of *Captain Marvel*. The word "fan" comes from "fanatic." Dedicated, opinionated, and fierce, Nancy Baym differentiates "fans" from "audiences" by characterizing their level of feeling about a media text, arguing that "fans feel for feeling's own sake" (2018, 81). This depth of feeling, emotion, and meaning-making creates a unique type of media viewer. And in public-facing venues like social media platforms, fans both participate and perform. In posting on a site like Twitter, for example, fans want to be seen having opinions and engaging in activities or collections. By participating in hype—by defending their favorite film, character, or comic book—they get enjoyment but also help perpetuate the success of the corporations that make money off them and the franchises they so enjoy.

For Pippa, reading the tweets felt messy at times because she was both a researcher and a fan of the *Captain Marvel* comics, characters, and films. She grappled with her coding strategy and her connections to the material as she read through thousands of tweets. Did her knowledge of the context add nuance to the manual coding of sentiments in the datasets? Or was she still beholden to objectivity when it came to evaluating computational sentiment analysis systems? Or did the outliers carry more weight for her than the gold standard annotations that form the basis of computational systems because of her deep ties to the subject matter? Drawing from data feminism (D'Ignazio and Klein 2020), in which researchers include themselves and their experiences in the work, through data fluencies we can see that both arguments need to be held together in order to grasp a more nuanced picture.

Pippa's coding strategies re-act to her data with nuance and subtlety, respecting contexts and histories. She understands that a tweet might be negative and positive all at once. A tweet's truncated form might respond to decades of narrative in a franchise and to volumes of fanfiction. VADER reacts differently, flattening a tweet that mixes positive and negative sentiments into the neutral category. When Pippa or the women in Cicero re-act, they rewrite and reclaim the scripts they're given.

As we have seen, corporate sentiment analysis techniques reduce the messy, embodied registers of feeling and emotion to quantified and quantifiable data and are often unable to process or compute the many ways our lives are bound up with systemic yet personal experiences of economic precarity, sexism, racism, homophobia and other oppressive forces. Machine and technocentric systems strip emotions and sentiments of their contexts and presume an ahistorical world in which identities, words, and meanings must slot into hollow categories. Then they are used to make decisions *about us* based on these flawed understandings and hollow categories. In contrast—as we'll see in the next chapter—humanities scholarship has grappled with emotion and affect quite differently. Data fluencies take seriously the messiness of living. 

## Notes

1 Lexicon-based sentiment analysis uses lists that connect certain words with specific emotions to determine the overall sentiment of text containing different vocabularies and phrases (Hutto and Gilbert 2014; Ribeiro et al. 2016).

2 "Karen" is a slang term that emerged in the United States in recent years as a shorthand for an entitled, usually white, female customer who frequently demands to "speak to the manager" when interacting with service employees. The meme first originated in response to several racially charged interactions in which middle-aged white women were recorded belittling, yelling at, or calling the police on Black people in public (Bhasin et al. 2020; Brady et al. 2023; Dubrofsky 2022).

## References


Adams, Philippa R. 2023. "Higher Further Faster: Social Media Discourses of Feminism, Misogyny, and *Captain Marvel*." PhD diss., Simon Fraser University. https://summit.sfu.ca/item/36445.

Albrecht, Carina, and Wendy Hui Kyong Chun. 2024. "The Digital Market of Interests and Feelings." In *Politics of Curiosity*, edited by Yves Citton and Enrico Campo. Routledge.

Aware. 2023a. "Revealed: The Surprising Cause of Worker Turnover." https://www.awarehq.com/blog/the-surprising-cause-of-worker-turnover.

Aware. 2023b. "The Retail Workplace Trends Report: What Frontline Workers Care About." https://www.awarehq.com/research/the-retail-workplace-trends-report.

Baym, Nancy. 2018. *Playing to the Crowd: Musicians, Audiences, and the Intimate Work of Connection*. NYU Press.

Bhasin, Tavishi, Charity Butcher, Elizabeth Gordon, Maia Hallward, and Rebecca LeFebvre. 2020. "Does Karen Wear a Mask? The Gendering of COVID-19 Masking Rhetoric." *International Journal of Sociology and Social Policy* 40 (9/10): 929–37. https://doi.org/10.1108/ijssp-07-2020-0293.

Brady, Miranda J., Erika Christiansen, and Emily Hiltz. 2023. "Good Karen, Bad Karen: Visual Culture and the Anti-Vaxx Mom on Reddit." *Journal of Gender Studies* 32 (6): 616–31. https://doi.org/10.1080/09589236.2022.2069088.

D'Ignazio, Catherine, and Lauren Klein. 2020. *Data Feminism*. MIT Press.

Donahue, Evan, Matthew Canute, Adjua Akinwumi, Philippa R. Adams, Maite Taboada, and Wendy Hui Kyong Chun. 2025. "Conflicting Feelings: Sociological and Computational Sentiment in Workplace Sentiment Surveillance." *AI & Society.* https://doi.org/10.1007/s00146-025-02600-7.

Dubrofsky, Rachel E. 2022. *Authenticating Whiteness: Karens, Selfies, and Pop Stars.* University Press of Mississippi.

Gregg, Melissa. 2018. *Counterproductive: Time Management in the Knowledge Economy.* Duke University Press.

Hutto, Clayton J., and Eric Gilbert. 2014. "VADER: A Parsimonious Rule-Based Model for Sentiment Analysis of Social Media Text." *Proceedings of the International AAAI Conference on Web and Social Media* 8 (1): 216–25. https://doi.org/10.1609/icwsm.v8i1.14550.

Ribeiro, Filipe N., Matheus Araújo, Pollyanna Gonçalves, Marcos André Gonçalves, and Fabrício Benevenuto. 2016. "SentiBench—a Benchmark Comparison of State-of-the-practice Sentiment Analysis Methods." *EPJ Data Science* 5 (1). https://doi.org/10.1140/epjds/s13688-016-0085-1.

Roethlisberger, Frederick J. 1941. *Management and Morale.* Harvard University Press.

[ 3 ]

# Counter

A teenage boy rolled through middle school in an intense bromance with his BFF. They built a deep reservoir of memes and jokes, spent countless weekends in each other's bedrooms immersed in video games, and developed their own shared lexicon and snarky sensibilities. Even in disagreements and temporary spats, they leaned into each other as they explored how they could shed their boyhood selves and become teens. They had so much in common; they seemed so similar, a perfect pair.

But high school cleaved them apart, spiraling them off to far-flung parts of their large city and different circles of friends. And as they began high school, the world around them was also changing. In 2016, Donald Trump won the US presidential election within a media environment that was increasingly dominated by social media platforms. Trump's election campaign benefited from earlier disruptions in the media ecosystem that allowed hate and conspiracies to spread, including the troll armies that drove the Gamergate[1] controversy beginning in 2014 and the Pizzagate[2] conspiracy theory that erupted on 4chan in 2016.

Halfway through Trump's first term, our young man reconnected with his friend, encountering him in a Discord chat as they gamed. Their reunion was energetic but short-lived. As they arranged to meet in person, the other boy casually announced, "By the way, you should probably know that my new friends and I are a little bit racist."

**As the first boy pushed to understand what this meant, it became clear his former friend had fallen down a far-right rabbit hole, largely fostered through online spaces that built on the lessons of Gamergate and Pizzagate to propagate white supremacy. Teens who shared so much, who had both grown up in a lefty West Coast neighborhood and who spent hundreds and hundreds of hours together on- and offline, quickly and easily veered into different and polarized worldviews despite their commonalities.**

This tale is not fictional. It draws from one of our team member's lives, an encounter that reoriented her research on digital media as she also helped her son grapple with the changes in his former friend. Over the last decade, and particularly since 2016, scholars have increasingly turned their attention to the proliferation of hate, misogyny, racism, and extremist recruiting online (Burton 2022; Donovan et al 2022; Phillips 2016). Various far-right groups have used platforms like Twitter, Facebook, YouTube, Discord, and Reddit (discussed in chapter 2) to mobilize events such as the Unite the Right Rally in Charlottesville, Virginia, in 2017 and the storming of the US Capitol in 2021. Groups like the Proud Boys, the Oathkeepers, and the Patriot Front share histories with twentieth-century white supremacist organizations, but there are also important differences (McPherson 2003). A new racial formation—with disturbingly fluid solidarity—is taking shape in the United States, one deeply bound up with the online platforms that have proliferated since 2004, and shifting figurations of race.

One of us (Tara) calls this new formation "immersive racism." Platforms like Discord, 8kun (previously 8chan), and Reddit can foster an intense experience of racism, steeping users in a toxic brew that easily flows across devices. Here, a new mode of explicit racism is celebrated, and the term "racist" is repackaged as a badge of honor. It's not a problem to be "a little bit racist" or proudly white; it's a way to identify yourself, a way to find community, a way to be a (white) man. Users try on racism, easing into its expression

[Figure 3.1]. Members of far-right extremist groups participating in the 2017 Unite the Right Rally in Charlottesville, Virginia. https://commons.wikimedia.org/w/index.php?curid=68193094. Photo by Anthony Crider; cropped by Beyond My Ken (talk) 20:37, April 9, 2018 (UTC), CC BY 2.0.

and deepening their commitments. They then emerge from these deep digital dives to infect other spaces—both on and offline—that seem relatively normal and that trade in the more covert racism from the 1990s.

It's not simply that these far-right groups *use* online platforms to mainstream their message and foment hate. Rather, the very design of these platforms encourages such turbulent activity. The anonymity of many sites encourages trolling and misinformation. The private ownership of platforms, their opaque algorithms, and a climate of widespread deregulation in the United States create fertile conditions for the spread of hate and fake news. Corporate social media platforms thrive on network effects—from increasing their user base, or the scalability we talked about in the introduction. Every use of a platform helps fuel its extractive business models. There is little incentive for a company to limit hate, for, in the logic of the platform, any use is good. Platforms' architectures and algorithms privilege content in particular ways that help hate to spread. As a result, hate speech should not be understood as a bug in the platform. It's a generative feature that extends the platform's reach and extractive capacities. We cannot disentangle the ubiquity of these platforms from the rapid expansion of white supremacist groups over the last twenty years.[3]

As chapter 1 reminds us, network architectures produce solidarities, some of which are surprising in their depth and breadth. These fluid solidarities can both enable and undermine social justice. Immersive racism deepens in vertical silos (the subreddit, the closed Discord chat), but it also flows along horizontal axes, moving across platforms (through hashtags, links, and virality) and producing strange bedfellows that erupt into our physical world. Pro-Palestinian activists at UCLA witnessed such strange fluid solidarities in April 2024 as their peaceful encampment was violently attacked over several days by angry off-campus agitators. This mob was composed of self-professed Zionists who were joined by white supremacists, including Proud Boys chanting, "We will finish what Hitler started" (Razack et al. 2024). Surprising solidarities indeed.

A seemingly discrete story of a boy, who is "a little bit racist," joins a larger stream of hate on- and offline and unspools into many questions. How is the political environment in the United States increasingly interlaced with digital platforms? How are race and gender reconfigured in a digital age? How might we understand the pull of extremist networks on young white men? What would *countering* this spreading hate look and feel like? What else might men be?

## All the Feels

As we saw in chapter 2, corporate sentiment analysis techniques reduce the messy, embodied registers of feeling and emotion to quantified and quantifiable data, often unable to process or compute the many ways our lives are bound up with systemic yet personal experiences of sexism, racism, homophobia, and other oppressive forces. The corporate reliance on LLMs, algorithms, and other large-scale data systems and models flatten the human experience while also making it easier to be a little bit (or a large bit) racist online. 

Our disconnects and our beliefs are deeply *felt*, signaling that we need to attend to how emotion and affect profoundly shape online engagements and immersive racism. Humanities scholarship has grappled with emotion and affect for decades. Scholars like Sara Ahmed have theorized the complexity of affect (related to but not the same as emotion), noting that "affect is what sticks, or what . . . preserves the connection between ideas, values, and objects" (2010, 29). Affect then unspools from "the messiness of the experiential, the unfolding of bodies into worlds, and the drama of contingency, how we are touched by what we are near" (30).

Because of this, there is no easy technological fix to dampen the tides of immersive racism. The last decade has provided ongoing evidence of the difficulties involved in countering mis- and disinformation. Scholarship has repeatedly shown that countering misinformation with factual corrections at best produces "effects [that] are often modest, decay relatively quickly, and fail to cumulate into sustained decreases in many common misperceptions" (Nyhan 2021). In some cases, attempts to debunk disinformation directly can instead solidify belief in false information. Beyond the academic research, we see the difficulty of countering misinformation every day across our media ecosystems, as conspiracy theories about pedophile-run pizza joints or fears of vaccines proliferate.

Across the various labs and projects that comprise Data Fluencies, we resist the Silicon Valley assumptions that technology will solve our problems. Indeed, we understand that technologies can often create problems, such as the proliferation of hate. While we are building computational tools, making digital media, and creating online networks, we nonetheless begin our work with our messy, complex multidimensional world. We counter techno-solutionism, recognizing that traditional conceptions of countering can produce unintended consequences.

Data fluencies take seriously the messiness of living. We conceived of the overarching project as a way to counter the impacts of mis- and disinformation on our data-filled world and to imagine *feeling* differently. From creating new tools for mixed qualitative-quantitative research to countering the spread of misleading and discriminatory information, we aim to amplify and foster multi-vocality, in solidarity with various communities and activist and student voices.

But might we think of countering differently? How might countering offer different flows of affect or emotion, different opportunities for cooperation, play, or co-creation? If conventional forms of countering rarely stanch the flow of conspiracy theories, if sentiment analysis repeatedly misinterprets our feelings, what other avenues might we pursue? How might our expanded conceptions of countering point us toward other ways of intervening within media ecosystems, even toward other ways of feeling and being?

The word "counter" has many meanings. The most common might lead us to a counterargument or to countering an attack, a defensive reaction that blocks an idea or a threat. As the previous chapter has shown, corporations counter the resistance of workers with obfuscating sentiment analysis. You might try to counter your mother's vaccine fears with scientific explanations. But there are other ways to approach a counter. Historically, we might think of students in the United States taking a seat at segregated lunch counters in the late 1950s. They were certainly countering Jim Crow and white supremacy by occupying space, but they did not directly engage the angry white mobs surrounding their protest, even as these mobs grew violent. Their strategy was resistant and defiant even as it ignored the mocking white mob, modeling a different way of feeling and staging a supportive relation between the protestors themselves. Similarly, the students in pro-Palestinian encampments in early 2024 had a policy of nonengagement with counterprotestors. Their focus was elsewhere: on Gaza, mutual care, and justice.

Could we learn from such techniques and stage the countering of immersive racism by attending to affect and different kinds of alliance? Can we imagine a counterintuitive approach to countering? Can we work upstream, thinking about how to build protection and taking small steps toward that end? Can we develop a habit of protection, daily rituals to mitigate and block harm?

There are many things we want to counter across the scope of our work together, including fascist recruiting; polarization; toxic masculinity; corporate exploitation; loneliness; racism; and other oppressions. We also want to counter the idea that technology will save us, that quantification will resolve any of these ills and tensions. Our countering is preventive but also generative and capacious. Instead of searching for one big solution, it embraces many small techniques for harm reduction—understanding the human, the material, and the digital to exist in deep relation.

To engage these questions, we turn to one small endeavor in imagining countering anew. This example shows how we build new fluencies in countering to help us imagine a world that is not inherently harmful—by multiplying joy but also lingering with pain.

## What's Up with Dudes? Emergent Process and Reclaiming Masculinity

As we've seen, neofascists, Christian nationalists, and other denizens of the far right are not shy about mobilizing digital platforms for their goals. Lurking in environments where young men go to alleviate their pain, loneliness, and frustrations about women and work, they offer solace and community. They actively blend online recruitment with real-world activities, from leafleting campaigns on campuses to the attack on the US Capitol in January 2021.

But the far right has no monopoly on digital networks or on providing solace for pain. Movement and fluency can go in many directions. Pain can find its way to fascism, but it can also forge

[Figure 3.2]. The Reclaim Project website. Source: The Reclaim Project.

whole new worlds and, as we have seen, surprising solidarities. We can practice harm reduction in relation to fascism, countering polarization through subtle protective eddies that build resilience, joy, and community.

One such testbed for imagining solidarity is the Reclaim Project, located in the University of Southern California's Sidney Harman Academy for Polymathic Study, a space open to all students regardless of major.[4] Guided by media fellow Ines Novačić, Dr. Curtis Fletcher, and Tara, the project aims not only to study and understand immersive racism in an academic register (i.e., through scholarly research and writing) but also to offer online alternatives to the violence and racism of the "manosphere." Since attempts at debunking disinformation often serve to paradoxically reinforce it, the Reclaim Project works in a different way. By identifying the friction points and emotions that often make young people susceptible to far-right recruitment, we situate our efforts upstream in the media ecosystem, offering alternatives for young people within the vernacular forms where they often have fluency: social media. We believe that young people can help us design better narratives to counter white nationalism both online and in the fleshy, messy human world. Its purpose is to move whiteness beyond grievance, anger, and guilt toward rich alliances across differences and emerging solidarities.

The project draws from Tara's earlier creative work and recent writing on emergent strategies by adrienne maree brown and Ruha Benjamin, discussed in the introduction to this book.[5] Emergent strategies differ from the top-down methods often used in organizing, instead favoring a more process-based approach. Emergent practices are adaptive, nonlinear, and iterative. They are situated locally and value deeply relational practices that are also decentralized. They learn from the natural world and the imaginative power of Indigenous cosmologies. They help us move the humanities from describing and analyzing crises to envisioning the world beyond crises, often in dialogue with the arts, community organizing, and mutual care.

As the far right shows us, emergent strategies are not a panacea or a turnkey solution: They also don't have a fixed political valence. Andrea Ritchie notes that Christian nationalists are operating their own emergent strategies right now. But she also reminds us that we begin by beginning. Faced with problems that resonate globally and seem intractable, she insists, following anti-violence activist Shannon Perez-Darby, that "all we need to do is ask ourselves, 'Can we create something better than this?'" (2023, 40).

The Reclaim Project answers Perez-Darby's call, working closely with groups of students since mid-2023. The students who make up the project are a highly heterogeneous group, drawn from many disciplines and many demographics. They are undergraduates, MAs and PhDs. The group has organized their work in interwoven threads: a research core, a design team, a strategy group, and a production team. Membership in these pods shifts and morphs, but the students are consistently given a high degree of autonomy and flexibility. Novačić, Fletcher, and Tara have provided a series of questions, initial research materials, and ongoing opportunities for dialogue, but the students are actively shaping the routes we travel. The initial process focused on understanding the feelings

[Figure 3.3]. A zine created by the Reclaim Team explaining our work. Source: The Reclaim Project.

and emotions driving the rise of online hate and white nationalism while also making sense of the rhythms of online platforms and the influencers that inhabit them. The group also spent time talking about how to protect oneself in such research, both technologically and mentally.

Through a slow and iterative process, they settled on how they would approach "countering" differently. Instead of addressing the Andrew Tates of the world directly, the students are focusing on what it means to be a man today, offering models of masculinity that don't spin into toxicity, ethnonationalism, and hate. As part of their work, they are cataloging progressive male influencers; organizing focus groups on campus to explore what masculinity means to students; and making media including "men on the street" interviews, a popular social media genre, and other formats such as a short documentary featuring a young man who escaped

[Figure 3.4]. Screengrab from the short documentary *Ctrl-Alt-Right,* completed by the Reclaim Project in 2025. Source: The Reclaim Project.

the pull of the manosphere. They are also using this social media production and influencer research in the development of a LLM and a detection model examining masculinity. They are experimenting with chat-driven and narrative gaming formats as well.

The students are learning from and building relationships with social media influencers, exploring the influencers' own data fluencies. For example, they have studied Twitch streamer Hasan Piker's construction of masculinity. While his streaming focuses on progressive news content and political analysis, his Instagram features his workouts and basketball obsession alongside his daily "fits" and his worries about weight gain. He offers a masculinity that is both virile and slightly vulnerable, a combination that has amassed a following of 2.8 million and has proven effective in moving young men away from right-wing rabbit holes. In September 2024, Reclaim brought Hasan to USC for a conversation with Tara about Twitch, politics, and masculinity. He spoke to a full house of over five hundred students, live streaming on his channel to over twenty-five thousand. A YouTube video of the event has reached over 276,000 views. Hasan's own strategy of countering leans

[Figure 3.5]. Hasan Piker (a.k.a. Hasanabi on Twitch) and his producer Marche visited USC and the Reclaim Project in September 2024 for a livestream and a lab visit. Source: The Reclaim Project. Photo by Robert Knaack.

heavily into a chat-driven version of media and political analysis that draws from popular culture and is often humorous. He was the only left-leaning influencer among the top ten most-viewed streams on election day in the United States in 2024, bringing in 7.5 million viewers over the night. The Reclaim team is examining his modes of address, learning strategies for countering far-right messaging in online spaces.

Many students also adore we_love_you, two young men with a following of 2.2 million on Instagram but serving a very different vibe. Channeling filmmaker Wes Anderson and a soft-hued aesthetic, they showcase a quirky model of male friendship, wonder, and connection to the natural world. Their version of being a man is kind, calming, and infused with optimism. Their friendship is an antidote to the story that started this chapter.

The Reclaim process is deeply collaborative and often messy. It may explore a path and loop back to try something new. Some trails are dead ends. But explorations such as these open us all up to more vibrant visions of a world to come. Reclaim offers alternatives—alternatives for the students who are learning to engage with these ideas, as well as for those who view the lively

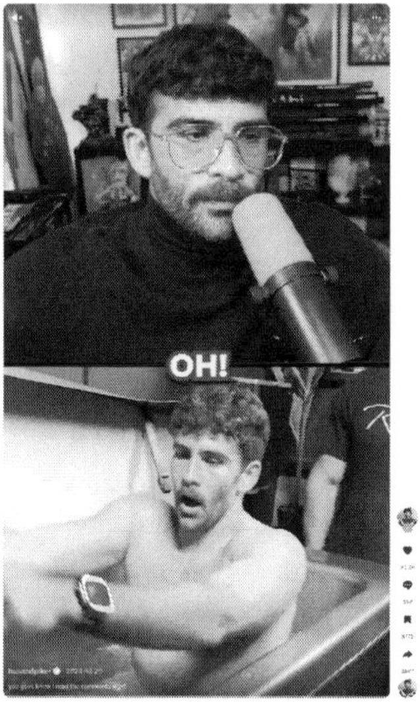


[Figure 3.6]. Hasan Piker responds to a video of himself getting into a cold tank, an image that combines his commentator self with a thirst-trap. Source: Piker's TikTok (hasanpiker).

[Figure 3.7]. The we_love_you social media accounts model a kinder #hopecore world of male friendship. Source: _we loveyou_'s TikTok.

media they are producing. These modes of countering are often oblique and subtle, but they open up new registers of masculinity online, seeding new fluencies. Reclaim meets both students and audiences where they are, valuing their engagements and frustrations with digital media, embracing co-creation yet also critique. The media the students produce may seem like droplets in the vast sea of content they join. Yet, as Ruha Benjamin reminds us, we need not only pursue the "grand, official, and codified." Rather, "a microscopic vision of justice and generosity, love, and solidarity can have exponential effects" (2022, 11).

Across this chapter, we have insisted that technology is not our savior. Social media often spirals into toxicity and immersive racism, fueling hate on- and offline. But as the Kara Keeling quotation in the introduction reminds us, these systems can also offer glimmers of other worlds, pulling us into surprising solidarities and imagining more generous ways of being. They are places to play with alternatives; with the way we are called to interact with various communities and threads in the stream of social media data. As the creators of we_love_you remind us, we are big and we are small. We contain multitudes; we might even have the potential to counter hate with joy.

## Notes

1 Gamergate was a sustained attack on women in the videogame industry in 2014. What proponents argued started with a defense of ethics in video game journalism spiraled into unchecked weaponized misogyny throughout nerd-adjacent online spaces that reverberates to this day (Blodgett 2020; Salter 2018).

2 Pizzagate is a conspiracy theory claiming that prominent leaders of the Democratic Party in the United States are engaged in a child-trafficking operation run out of the basement of a Washington, DC, pizzeria (Aisch et al. 2016).

3 The Southern Poverty Law Center provides one set of data on the expansion of white supremacist organizations. Their report on 2023 notes that there was a 50 percent surge in these groups in that year alone, the biggest leap ever recorded by the SPLC. They also document 143 white power and neo-Nazi rallies in 2023. Different organizations offer slightly different data on the resurgence of white supremacist organizations over the past twenty years, but all document a notable increase. Of course, white supremacy exists in myriad forms beyond organized extremist groups as well, as it long has.

4 See The Reclaim Project, https://www.thereclaimproject.net/.

5 Tara's collaborative practice in difference and design is chronicled in her book *Feminist in a Software Lab* (2018). Learn more about the Harman Academy here: https://polymathic.usc.edu/.

## References

Ahmed, Sara. 2010. "Happy Objects." In *The Affect Theory Reader,* edited by M. Gregg and G. J. Seigworth. Duke University Press.

Aisch, Gregor, Jon Huang, and Cecilia Kang. 2016. "Dissecting the #PizzaGate Conspiracy Theories." *New York Times,* December 10. https://www.nytimes.com/interactive/2016/12/10/business/media/pizzagate.html.

Benjamin, Ruha. 2022. *Viral Justice: How We Grow the World We Want.* Princeton University Press.

Blodgett, Bridget. 2020. "Media in the Post #GamerGate Era: Coverage of Reactionary Fan Anger and the Terrorism of the Privileged." *Television and New Media* 21 (2): 184–200. https://doi.org/10.1177/1527476419879918.

brown, adrienne maree. 2017. *Emergent Strategy: Shaping Change, Changing Worlds.* AK Press.

Burton, Anthony G. 2022. "Blackpill Science: Involuntary Celibacy, Rational Technique, and Economic Existence Under Neoliberalism." *Canadian Journal of Communication* 47 (4): 676–701. https://doi.org/10.3138/cjc.2022-07-25.

Donovan, Joan, Emily Dreyfuss, and Brian Friedberg. 2022. *Meme Wars: The Untold Story of the Online Battles Upending Democracy in America.* Bloomsbury Publishing.

McPherson, Tara. 2003. *Reconstructing Dixie: Race, Gender, and Nostalgia in the Imagined South.* Duke University Press.

McPherson, Tara. 2018. *Feminist in a Software Lab: Difference + Design.* Harvard University Press.

Nyhan, B. 2021. "Why the Backfire Effect Does Not Explain the Durability of Political Misperceptions." *Proceedings of the National Academy of Sciences—PNAS* 118 (15): 1–7.

Phillips, Whitney. 2016. *This Is Why We Can't Have Nice Things: Mapping the Relationship Between Online Trolling and Mainstream Culture.* MIT Press.

Razack, Sherene, Gaye Theresa Johnson, Robin D. G. Kelley, Shannon Speed, Saree Makdisi, and Ali Behdad. 2024. "What Does Anti-Arab Racism on Campus Have to Do with the War on Gaza?" *The Nation,* May 23. https://www.thenation.com/article/archive/ucla-anti-arab-racism-palestinian-rights/.

Ritchie, Andrea. 2023. *Practicing New Worlds: Abolition and Emergent Strategies.* AK Press.

Salter, Michael. 2017. "From Geek Masculinity to Gamergate: The Technological Rationality of Online Abuse." *Crime Media Culture an International Journal* 14 (2): 247–64. https://doi.org/10.1177/1741659017690893.

Southern Poverty Law Center. n.d. "The Year in Hate & Extremism 2023." https://www.splcenter.org/resources/year-hate-extremism-2023.

[ 4 ]

# Play

Have you ever entered a space (both digital and IRL) dedicated to games or play and wondered, "Wow—why is it so unimaginative or stupid? Why am I play-cooking in high heels? Why am I pretending to be a mass shooter? Why am I buying burgers to get prizes I don't really want? Why do I have to solve this math problem before I can play?"

The limits and damages of this restriction of play hit one of us (Gillian) when she took her child, Finn, to Kidtropolis for the first time. Kidtropolis sells itself as "the perfect environment for parents and caregivers to bond with their children by participating together in pretend play"—a space where kids can use their imagination to explore future possibilities (Kidtropolis n.d.).

She remembers that, as she entered the space, she thought that it would be a great way to spend a morning with her four-year-old son. It was quite remarkable: a miniature city, complete with child-sized replicas of a bank, hospital, construction site, police station, airport, and restaurant, buzzing with tiny citizens who were dutifully taking on their roles. Finn's eyes were wide with excitement when he was handed a small, laminated ID badge declaring him a "citizen" of this pint-sized world, along with instructions that he could be anything he wanted—a doctor, a business owner, a firefighter, even a chef. She watched as he sprinted off to eagerly become a member of the labor force.

> Watching him mimic the actions of a doctor, pilot, and policeman, she realized how much these activities mirrored adult responsibilities. The experience of Kidtropolis seemed to exemplify the idea that our world is crafted with paths already laid out for us, a place where children are gently nudged into roles society has long inscribed for them.
>
> She found herself constantly asking: In a space where anything is possible, why is it that they replicate the same old things?
>
> While we recognize the value and importance of these spaces for youth development, we trouble the notion that places like Kidtropolis are spaces where youths use their imagination to create future possibilities. It is, in fact, the exact opposite of an imagination space. At Kidtropolis, children were being taught to *play in place.* They weren't "just" playing; they were being subtly trained to fit into the roles that sustain the modern laboring society. It's a model of life based on the logic of "productive play," whereby play constrains rather than nurtures possibility.

So how do we nurture and develop ourselves in play that opens rather than constrains our imagination? How might we *play out of place*?

Camp Kiki, run by one of us (Kishonna) at the University of Kentucky, enacts such playing out of place, creating turbulent spaces for care and solidarity—in which we counter and rewrite, rather than follow, the scripts we're given through play. This camp hosts a group of under-resourced youths from the Central Kentucky and Appalachian regions.

The one-week program advertised itself as a space to play video games and become e-sports competitors. But the students who took part, having had prior experience with STEM camps that lure students in with games (while only reserving very little time for play for play's sake), assumed Camp Kiki would be the same "bait and switch." The students did end up learning some history, crafting narratives, engaging in conflict resolution and peer mediation, and even exploring the maker spaces in the College of Engineering—but through actual play.

As Kishonna recalls:

At first, the campers hemmed and hawed. Hoodies up. Eyes down. Until play began.

That first day they set the tone and template for how they would engage through a round of Smash Bros, a platform fighting game. They were put into pairs for a two-versus-two battle. The first round was a free-for-all—just to see how they would interact with each other. Kishonna knew they would be trash-talking, cursing, being mean, bullying, and engaging in other forms of antisocial behavior. It's normal. (Sadly.)

Before they went to round two, they were very comfortable with each other. Although their parents and teachers might not have approved, Kishonna allowed cursing. She allowed them the ability to express themselves in ways that might not have been allowed in school. But she did address another concern.

She asked them: "There are two types of people in the world, builders and destroyers. Which one are you?"

They looked at her, confused at first. So she repeated, "Based on the first round of play, would you consider yourself a builder or a destroyer? A builder uplifts—a destroyer puts down."

She felt the shame wash over them. Some put their eyes back down. Some put the hoodies back up over their heads. They were recalling what their grannies and mamas had told them: "Be on your best behavior. Remember your home training. Don't embarrass me or yourself."

They had all been told some variation of that self-correction—which went out the window when gaming started. After a few moments of sitting silently, allowing the shame to punish them and public humiliation to humble them, a voice from the crowd emerged and responded: "From that game? We are all destroyers. We didn't even uplift our teammate."

More silence.

They understood Kishonna's point. She didn't yell at them, chastise them, correct their behavior, belittle them, or even critique them. She instead allowed them to do it themselves. She even heard a small voice in the back say: "She gon' send me home. I was cussing!" Kishonna immediately assured everyone that they wouldn't be sent home. She wasn't even going to report them.

What she would do was give them a do-over. "How about a second round? Show me what it means to be a builder. Show me what it means to be a team. Let's build community. Because here at Camp Kiki, we believe in unlimited chances."

Eyes up. Hoodies off. They all went back to the consoles for the second round. But before they started, several of them talked about strategy. They coached each other and gave pointers and tips on how to counter a move. They came up with a plan.

The second round went much better than the first. It was still loud and boisterous, but there were many more prosocial engagements. The campers created their own ethic of care. They created a community.

After that round was over, Kishonna had the campers write down their own "rules of engagement"—a document outlining how they would conduct themselves over the week. They easily created it: "Take turns. Ask for help. Offer help. Trash talk is OK. Toxic behavior is not." The document was a manifesto of sorts. It was simple and to the point. It was created from the bottom up and developed organically.

When the campers returned the next day, the drop-off was completely different. They had already set the tone for a day of gaming and kept the guiding document in mind. They self-regulated. No one got kicked out. No one had to be seriously reprimanded. Play was the motivating factor; it was not the reward for good behavior. Unlike in Kidtropolis, the play was not the problem.

While we intrinsically understand this concept, we wanted to also apply concepts from social work and engineering to our play experiences, to see what the world of "building with care looked like." It might sound like a corny joke (a social worker, engineer, and mom walk into a bar type stuff), but we truly gathered and brought the best of play to the space. The social work brought care and concern, and engineering brought concept and creation, and both perspectives have been informative to imagine what worlds could be built. These data fluencies are necessary as creation and building are not done in isolation.

While the focus of Camp Kiki would not even fit the definition of a STEM camp, what the researchers observe is that the basic tenets of most of our disciplines (humanities included) are already present in the everyday things that we do as people. We take for granted that we engage in science, technology, and magic every day. Take Kishonna's mom. When she would prepare Sunday meals, the kitchen would take different forms. In one moment, it would appear to be a homely and quaint village set up with fresh fruits and vegetables ready to blend with others to create fusions from across the diasporas. In another moment, mom appeared to be a chemist in her lab tinkering with fire and liquids to create something from nothing. But at the core of both is curiosity and care for others—a blending or, rather, fusion of social work and engineering.

## Play in Place; Learn What I Say

Coming from play scholars, it might sound strange for us to say that "play is a problem." But given how play is operationalized, or gamified, within societal structures, it is clear that play *is* a problem. On the surface, it would seem that society believes in the power and potential of play—but only, as Kidtropolis and most STEM camps make clear, if it leads to productive workers. Play can serve as a training ground for perpetuating the roles and hierarchies of the past. But it doesn't have to be this way. As Kishonna's experience with Camp Kiki makes clear, play can also be the way out—but only if we move from "play in place" toward "playing out of place."

We've long identified what humans' basic needs are. Beyond food and shelter, other items are luxuries or byproducts of capitalistic societies. One of the basic needs that we have collectively neglected is play, which some assume is the opposite of work. So, if we indulge in more play then we have not completed our fair share of work (speaking in very agrarian and pastoral types of cultures, not capitalistic ones). But the opposite of work is not play and is in fact pleasure. And we need to begin to recultivate our basic need for play. What we have done is put "play in place."

To "play in place" is to follow a command. The dominant "play in place" model emphasizes learning topics, themes, and skills for work. We get rewarded for taking care of our virtual home, for being a loyal shopper, and for killing as many enemy combatants as possible. Play in place damages ourselves and our planet—repetitive strain injuries, voracious capitalist accumulation, individualism, and so on.

This collapse of work and play is everywhere, especially in education, where games become a "carrot" to reward students—or teaching itself becomes gamified. This is particularly rampant in STEM: Every school has a Coding Camp, Coding for Girls, Girls in STEM, and so on, which all focus on games as a way to foster interest in STEM subjects. To be clear, we are not arguing that games for learning are necessarily a bad thing—but we wonder what happens when gaming is constrained in this way, and teaching becomes analogous to breaking in horses.

Crucially, many teachers say that games for learning, especially around math and science, don't adequately replace traditional instruction. iPads, computers, and technology in general are mostly underutilized in traditional classrooms (Mosley 2013; Graham et al. 2020). And because there are only a handful of programs and applications that students are allowed to use, most of them are hard to learn and the other ones perform poorly (Famularsih 2020; Reich 2020).

In interviews, Kishonna asked teachers why these tools are inadequate and unused. They stated that learning them takes up too much time—and they are already strapped for time navigating the professional development model their schools require them to follow, sentiments expressed in the literature as well (Famularsih 2020; Reich 2020). Teachers are already dramatically underpaid for their work, so adding more layers and tools for them to incorporate in the classroom in a sustained way (as more than a quick reward) becomes an insurmountable challenge, especially if they need to control the class.[1]

It's not just in games for education. The collapsing together of work and play has also infiltrated traditional gaming spaces, where there is now an aspect of labor present—working toward opening something, unlocking something, and reaching some particular achievement. The game's imperative requires and forces you to have to work to take advantage of the luxuries of the game.

This is also where data fluencies contributes to understanding of play and games. One of the core sources of energy for humans is through play. Work takes our energy, so a social work perspective helps us understand that humans need relief from work and resources to support that relief.

## Freeing Play

The construction of play or leisure as a reward for labor recalls leisure's troubling and emancipatory history. Historically, leisure has been reserved for elite classes, as a form of freedom essential for their cultivation. It was made possible, though, by exploiting the work of others, who were condemned as lazy if they recreated,[2] especially since play always carries an undercurrent of freedom.

Tellingly, in response to a query to narrate some of the pastimes and sports he had engaged in, Booker T. Washington in *Up from Slavery* notes, "until that question was asked it had never occurred to me that there was no period of my life that was devoted to play. From the time that I can remember anything, almost every day of my life has been occupied in some kind of labour; though I think I would now be a more useful man if I had had time for sports" (1901, 237).

Similarly, W. E. B. Du Bois—with whom Booker T. Washington famously disagreed on many topics—suggested that educators had a special responsibility to ensure ample time away from work and labor for the overall well-being of the body politic, especially to develop the South and Black folks post-slavery. "We must rapidly come to the place," he argued, "where the man—all brain and no muscle is looked upon as almost as big a fool as the man—all muscle and no brain" (1897, 236). Du Bois did not just emphasize the need to balance sports and reading; he also stressed the need for games like billiards. Critiquing the YMCA's condemnation of billiards, Du Bois suggested that it could have some benefit if it was not conflated with gambling and drinking (1897, 231).

These arguments for the power of recreation trouble the traditional separation of working from the "leisure classes" (Veblen [1899] 2007) and refuse to see Black, Indigenous, and immigrant leisure as "laziness." As thinkers like Max Weber (as cited in Jacobsen 2018) and Adam Smith ([1776] 2002) have suggested, conversations of laziness and idleness increased when immigrant workers and formerly enslaved populations entered the traditional workforce. It was these narratives of laziness that propelled a national conversation to essentially shame folks into working for poverty wages and in atrocious working conditions. These narratives also led to reenslavement. Post-reconstruction, when Du Bois and Washington were writing, Black men were routinely imprisoned for "vagrancy"—condemning them to work on chain gangs and plantations (Keese 2014).

The reduction of play to work exemplified by Kidtropolis and some games for education thus perverts one of the most important reasons to respect play: freedom—but undercurrents of freedom still course through. To make this point, we return to Washington's comments on leisure. Although he frames his comments as play in terms of becoming more "useful," his statement reveals how play opens the future. By contemplating play, he imagines a different reality for himself.

Play for us belongs to this realm of "futures": *imagining new roles and ways of being and rewriting the script of what is possible in the world.* It is something through which different norms, structures, rules, and cultures may emerge. Play, we show, has the opportunity to offer a way to re-act to, counter, and escape the pre-scripted and preconstructed world.

## Play out of Place

So, again, what does "playing out of place" that amplifies rather than dampens freedom look like?

To answer this question, we return to Camp Kiki to unpack the power of gaming on education. As you'll recall from the previous example, the campers created their own rules of engagement by reflecting on their free play—a first step to playing out of place.

To play out of place, we need to overcome structures of assessment and control, which restrain student imaginations—but doing so is hard. The campers' engagement with LARPing (Live-Action Role Play) shows this nicely. Unlike in the Kidtropolis example, which placed kids in an already constructed place, here students were responsible for building their own weapons, designing and constructing their costumes, and building a set. Many initially wanted to know if they would fail, or what their grades would be if they created their stories, characters, and costumes in the "wrong" way. These students had adopted a deficit model—that if they didn't do something well to the team's liking, they wouldn't pass. It became an uphill battle trying to get students to reintroduce their natural imaginative capacities for making, creating, and doing. In a multiday process, they began working on creating their story alongside their LARP leader, Ed Chang, an English professor at Ohio University. Chang guided the students down a path of rediscovering who they were, and the activities created a high degree of confidence. The students demonstrated their creative skills for storytelling, narrative, and character development.

Many parents and teachers thought that this degree of freedom and playing would lead to destructive and disrespectful behaviors. They thought that to manage a classroom, you had to be in control because otherwise there could be no learning. This is why games are usually framed as a reward for good behavior—a way to buttress a teacher's control. But in fact, Camp Kiki's gentle teaching approach led to the opposite. Many students indicated that they had better emotional regulation because they now felt empowered.

Kishonna's point is that to learn, we need to dismantle the need for power, control, and domination. Once this was clear to everyone involved, it led to more collaborative creation spaces, fluid spaces in which everyone learned, re-acted, and played together. By disrupting the traditional classroom instruction model, Kishonna and her team were able to see how play could lead to world-building—to rewriting, rather than following scripts.

This is not the end of the story; play is not the sole answer to all of our problems. But we can start with curiosity. With a willingness to step into the sandbox.

## Notes

1 When games are considered part of the curriculum, teachers tend to incorporate them only as a reward. For example, when Kishonna established the Camp Kiki Academy—an in-school gaming class in which consoles and gaming were

brought to a local high school every Tuesday—there was an initial conflict between Kishonna's team and the teacher. The teacher wanted to use the gaming program as a reward for good behavior and attendance during the week, but Kishonna disagreed. The gaming program was part of the curriculum and was not supposed to be dependent on other factors. The teacher suggested to Kishonna that gaming was a reward and that she wasn't going to budge. Kishonna gently countered that we would never say math is optional, or that a student couldn't attend school because they didn't finish their history homework. The Camp Kiki Academy is the same thing; each session builds off the previous one. Students build capacities for learning through the games they play each week. Kishonna thought this was a huge miss for students, but she wasn't in charge, so she couldn't change it. But many of the students suggested that incorporating more of these kinds of lessons into their curriculum was life-changing for them. It made coming to school worth it, knowing they would be able to attend Camp Kiki.

2 Aristotle framed leisure as the freedom to consciously engage in activities—outside the responsibilities of work, family, and society—for relaxation, diversion, or to broaden one's knowledge. It is a meaningful human experience that involves being in the moment, cultivating yourself, and connecting with other people. Aristotle also supported what he called "natural slavery"; he positioned thinking and free time with the master and physical labor with the slave.

## References


Du Bois, W. E. B. (1897) 1980. "The Problem of Amusement." In *W.E.B. DuBois on Sociology and the Black Community.* University of Chicago Press.

Famularsih, Sari. 2020. "Students' Experiences in Using Online Learning Applications Due to COVID-19 in English Classroom." *Studies in Learning and Teaching* 1 (2): 112–21. https://doi.org/10.46627/silet.v1i2.40.

Graham, Marien Alet, Gerrit Stols, and Ruan Kapp. 2020. "Teacher Practice and Integration of ICT: Why Are or Aren't South African Teachers Using ICTs in Their Classrooms." *International Journal of Instruction* 13 (2): 749–66. https://doi.org/10.29333/iji.2020.13251a.

Kidtropolis. n.d. "About Kidtropolis Company—Kidtropolis." https://www.kidtropolis.ca/about-us.

Jacobsen, Michael Hviid. 2018. "Laziness: From Medieval Sin to Late Modern Social Pathology." In *Emotions, Everyday Life and Sociology.* Routledge.

Keese, Alexander. 2014. "Slow Abolition Within the Colonial Mind: British and French Debates about 'Vagrancy', 'African Laziness', and Forced Labour in West Central and South Central Africa, 1945–1965." *International Review of Social History* 59 (3): 377–407. https://www.jstor.org/stable/26394686.

Mosley, Vicky. 2013. "Qualitative Study: Why Technology Is Underutilized in K-12 Education." In *Society for Information Technology & Teacher Education International Conference.* Association for the Advancement of Computing in Education (AACE).

Reich, Justin. 2020. *Failure to Disrupt: Why Technology Alone Can't Transform Education.* Harvard University Press.

Smith, Adam. (1776) 2002. "An Inquiry into the Nature and Causes of the Wealth of Nations." *Readings in Economic Sociology*, 6–17.

Veblen, Thorstein. (1899) 2007. *The Theory of the Leisure Class: An Economic Study of Institutions.* Oxford University Press.

Washington, Booker T. 1901. *Booker T. Washington: Up from Slavery; An Autobiography.* A. L. Burt Company Publishers.

[ 5 ]

# [Sandbox]

The Intersectional Tech project at the University of Kentucky (and now, the University of Michigan) uses play to dismantle power, control, and domination, by allowing space and support to imagine new ways of being. Chapter 4 showed how these principles are enacted and shared with the wider community through Camp Kiki. Key to conceptualizing this type of play were concepts borrowed from engineering. Kishonna worked closely with engineer Ruth Imarhiagbe to define and redefine play through engineering.

For Imarhiagbe, play involves pleasure, fun, learning, relaxing, and socializing. Play is accessible to all ages and does not foreground practicality. It involves exercise, but for enjoyment not practicality, like the eddies and fluid solidarities in chapter 1, play thrives in and through movement.

We are all very familiar with the use of play in learning. Whether learning the ABCs while dancing to Cocomelon, reviewing lesson concepts on Kahoot!, or finally tackling Spanish on Duolingo, we have all been immersed in productivity through leisure. During Imarhiagbe's undergraduate studies in biomedical engineering, she often found herself recalling concepts in biology, chemistry, and math exams, with the help of songs taught to her back in middle school. There is no doubt that our memories are piqued when we approach difficult concepts through play (Yang and Chen 2021). Several fields of study use this idea of play for learning, including education, medicine, science, social science, engineering, and art.

But what if we flipped the switch? Instead of focusing our studies on how play can be used to improve learning—in this case engineering skills—what if we looked at how play could be improved solely for the sake of play *through* engineering? Play through engineering promotes play and leisure through creation and making. The fun of building and destroying and building again—sandcastles on the beach or in the sandbox as a kid.

## Designing Play

Video game production uses a wide range of product design and engineering skills. Creating a simple game like *Mario Party* requires the efforts of game designers, programmers, artists, level designers, software engineers, and many others. To contribute to the development process, these specialists use 2D and 3D design software, programming languages, and AI rendering tools—many of which are developed by engineers and computer scientists. In some cases, Nintendo, the makers of *Mario Party,* task their engineers with creating proprietary tools and software that are specifically designed to create their games. These proprietary tools also help safeguard the intellectual property of upcoming games. As we can see, engineering plays a crucial role in the creation of electronic and video games.

## Developing and Testing Play

In engineering, we talk about the *sandbox environment.* This might evoke images you're familiar with—children playing on the beach or in a dedicated sandbox. Packing sand together to form new structures, adding dimensions. An engineering sandbox is similar. In this case, engineers and developers interact with the software or device in an isolated environment during the development process. The goal is not to win or complete or accomplish, but to observe interactions in and with the environment, to create, to explore.

In the software sandbox the focus is on exploration: what *can* and what *is* co-created and discovered within? No answer is wrong, and the outcome is inconsequential, but by interacting with the software, developers explore the depth of possibilities that can be created with the tools they have. In this way, the mere development and testing of software can provide a source of play and imaginative creativity.

Sierra Thompson, a social worker with Kishonna's Intersectional Tech Project, offers that an open, sandbox environment provides a way to explore what humans do (when bothered and unbothered) and how things in the environment impact their realities. This was also a great way to see how much humans can rely on themselves for troubleshooting and how much humans might need others for support.

## Improving Health and Enhancing Gameplay

Whether players are engaging in leisure activities, competing as professional athletes, or participating in esports (electronic sports or video game tournaments), accidents and injuries are always possible. Injuries can result from the strenuous nature of play—think running at recess or playing football—or muscle wear from continuous repetitive motion such as using video game controllers or playing tennis. Engineering works on that too!

Biomedical engineers devote their knowledge of science, engineering, and product design to creating drugs, medical devices, exercise plans, and research methods to improve the quality-of-care doctors and therapists provide to patients. They also design the diagnosis, treatment, and therapy equipment used in hospitals, including syringes, X-ray and MRI machines, heart monitors, prosthetics, contact lenses, and glucose monitors.

One way play can be improved is through the development of better health routines and therapeutic devices that aid in pain alleviation, injury prevention, and the easy detection of root causes of ailments. Biomedical engineers also develop exercise devices that help players train and develop their intended skills. The faster a leisure or professional gamer is diagnosed and treated for game-related ailments, the sooner they can recover and return to playing more games.

In addition, like doctors, biomedical engineers spend significant time studying the anatomy of the human body. With this expertise, they design human-centered gaming devices such as controllers, keyboards, and mouses, as well as safety and comfort devices like knee pads, limb braces, and ergonomic chairs that contour to players' bodies and make gameplay easier, more streamlined, and more fun.

## Amateur Engineering: Building Hit Boxes

There is an indescribable sense of accomplishment that comes from creating one's source of play. Whether it is building and organizing a mini-Lego town to role-play your action figures in or building a pillow fort to snuggle up with family while playing board games, we can all attest to the joy we have felt getting to play with *and share* something we made with our own hands. This feeling was no different for JS, a friend and leisure gamer Imarhiagbe recently had the privilege of observing.

One day, Imarhiagbe entered the room to find JS leaning forward at the dining table, drill set in hand. There was an empty cigar

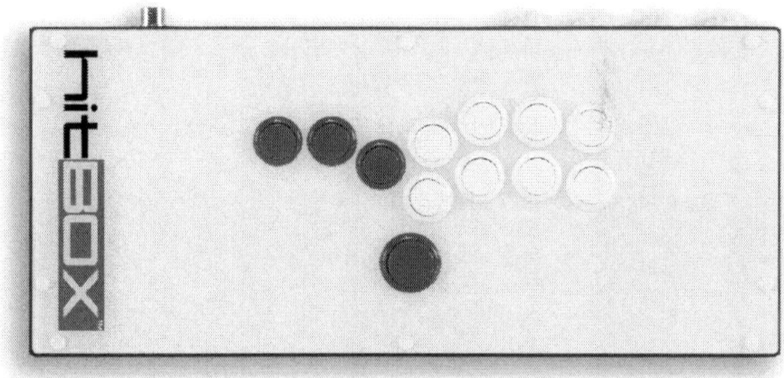


[Figure 5.1]. Official Hit Box. Source: The Original Hit Box Controller created by Shawn Huffer and Dustin Huffer; Official Hit Box (Hit Box Arcade 2025). https://www.hitboxarcade.com/products/hit-box.

box on the table and a printed stencil patterned with intentionally spaced holes. Spread out in front of him were several wires, a circuit board, and what looked like arcade push buttons. Walking closer, Imarhiagbe picked up a button and inquired as to what he was doing. He explained that he recently discovered he could make his own Hit Box—an innovative arcade-style controller specifically designed by Hit Box Arcade to enhance play in fighting games—and was trying to do so. His father had been able to find him a cigar box he could inexpensively reengineer, to serve as the base of his Hit Box.

Scholarship on gaming technologies inform us that accessibility in gaming is also deeply connected to capital (one must have money to participate and purchase things for that participation) (Gray, 2020). Usually, an official Hit Box retails for about $300 or more. However, players in the Fighting Game Community realized that with some creative thinking, they could source the important components and design themselves custom Hit Boxes, also known as leverless arcade sticks. In this example, DIY in gaming is a data fluency built upon creative and computational thinking to participate.

Not only do using these leverless arcade sticks bring joy and motivation to the players building and using them, but these gamers have gone beyond aesthetics, using the principles of engineering to design upgraded Hit Boxes and other controllers that support improved speed and precision of button inputs, thereby enhancing gamer performance (Juan 2024). They find issues with the current gaming technologies while playing and go to the drawing board to develop concepts and design products tailored to their gameplay style and the software's mechanics.

Fan innovations, like mods and custom controllers, also drive the overall improvement of gaming peripherals across the industry. Developers see tangible evidence of their game's reception by players, and more importantly, how these players creatively enhance their gameplay. This inspires the gaming industry to develop better

[Figure 5.2]. A DIY Wooden Leverless Arcade Stick Displaying Comic Scenes. Source: JUANminiDIY. https://juanminidiycom/, 2025.

hardware, software, and ergonomic features, further improving play for the public. In turn, these new features attract nonplayers who are either intrigued by the innovative designs created by their peers (like Imarhiagbe was) or are interested in the game's additions or modifications introduced by the industry.

Games—especially competitive team games—require teamwork, fulfilling the human need for connection and understanding. The use of engineering adds an extra layer of depth, not only within the gaming community but also across all the communities connected with the gamer. Ruth Imarhiagbe explains: When someone like JS wants to build their own version of a hit box, they first connect with others doing the same thing, seeking answers from fellow hobbyists, computer engineers, electricians, and his father (in this case). These are ways he connects to the world that he would not have if he were content with the base game or with simply saving up money to buy a consumer-grade hit box, instead of putting time and passion into making one of his own. So, in this case, engineering improves socialization and connection, which in turn improves opportunity for play.

As we continue to push the boundaries of engineering, opportunities for play will expand in ways we can only begin to imagine. By integrating advanced technologies, innovative design principles, and a deeper understanding of human interaction, engineering will unlock new dimensions of play that transcend traditional boundaries. In harnessing the power of engineering, we will create more immersive, engaging, and social experiences that benefit individual players and entire communities.

Data fluencies begin from the premise that everyone has something to contribute, and everyone can learn from each other. In these emancipatory learning environments, we are building the confidence and capacities to co-create, in real time, inside these spaces, as chapter 6 shows in more detail.

## References

Hit Box Arcade. n.d. "HIT BOX." Retrieved January 17, 2025, from https://www.hitboxarcade.com/products/hit-box.

Juan. 2024. "The Ultimate Guide to Customizing Your Hitbox Arcade Stick." JUANminiDIY, September 25. https://juanminidiy.com/the-ultimate-guide-to-customizing-your-hitbox-arcade-stick/.

Yang, K. H., and H. H. Chen. 2023. "What Increases Learning Retention: Employing the Prediction-Observation-Explanation Learning Strategy in Digital Game-Based Learning." *Interactive Learning Environments* 31 (6): 3898–3913.

[ 6 ]

# Co-Create

Before it landed in hot water for its involvement with Cambridge Analytica[1] (Confessore 2018), before its parent company changed its name to Meta (Dwoskin 2021), and before it faced an onslaught of criticism for knowingly inflicting harm on teenagers' mental health for the sake of profit[2] (Wells et al. 2021), Facebook found itself mired in controversy after it published an article that revealed that the company, in collaboration with researchers from Cornell, had played with users' feeds to determine whether users took on the emotional valences of the content to which they were exposed (Kramer et al. 2014).

The paper was based on an experiment conducted in 2012 on 689,003 Facebook users, which it referred to as "participants." In the experiment, Facebook frequently changed the content that these users were fed. Using sentiment analysis systems (described in chapter 2), this study, published in *Proceedings of the National Academy of Sciences* (PNAS), reported that users who saw positive content made happier posts; users who saw negative content were more likely to be negative. The authors claimed significance primarily due to the scale of the experiment (Kramer et al. 2014).

One of many problems: The targeted Facebook users didn't know they were participants. In the subsequent months, Facebook received a barrage of criticism about the questionable ethics of actively manipulating its users' feeds without their knowledge. The company argued that, by agreeing to its terms of service, users implicitly agreed to participate in any studies or experiments that Facebook's researchers might perform[3] (Meyer 2014). However, scholars argued that the study violated the core tenets of informed consent, integral to the academic research process since the mid-twentieth century (Flick 2016). PNAS eventually issued an expression of concern for the article, and Cornell revealed that its researchers did not have the experiment reviewed by the school's Institutional Review Board before it began (Carberry 2014)—raising substantial ethical concerns (Flick 2016).

Examining the fallout from this flawed research effort, one question becomes clear: How can someone "participate" in something if they don't know what they're participating in? The initial PNAS article calls the selected Facebook users "participants," but the participation the article authors refer to is passive at best. Such an approach is widespread. In the tech world, the "participant" is a tester: someone whose primary purpose is to engage with something that's already close to being done.

In the tech-world status quo, people and data are often treated like discrete, separable things. People are often said to "part with" their data when they engage with digital platforms and spaces, and that data is then used to predict, guide, or shape our future experiences both online and off. In these instances, the human is deprioritized in favor of the data—because, in many ways, one is much more easily commodified, manipulated, or controlled than the other.

Our data is thus often envisioned as a proxy for our personal, lived experiences. But as we saw in chapters 1 and 2, the data that is collected and analyzed only tells a part of the story; there are omissions, erasures, conflations, and distillations that necessarily occur for our data to shape the hyper-individualized experiences we have online. The decisions that are made for us in these spaces—the ads we see, the recommendations we receive, even (as Facebook attempted in 2012) the emotional registers of the posts we read—are based on assumptions about who we are and who we might become. The people providing the data on which these decisions are based have no say in the way their lives are mined, classified, and sorted, and often have no awareness of how their actions and experiences are used in the name of research or optimization. In other words, they don't know how they are participating in work that will deeply affect them down the line.

The Facebook study represents the extreme end of a warped perception of what participation has come to mean for the research and design process. In this paradigm, participants are objects and not subjects—they have studies conducted on them but have no say in the way those studies are designed or implemented. These practices maintain and strengthen power imbalances between the researcher and the researched. If this is how we are primed to think about participation in our tech-driven society, it's no wonder our technologies undertake invasive and nonconsensual extraction of our data.

So, how do we counter these practices? How do we involve communities in our work in more dialogical and reciprocal ways? How could data fluencies reimagine the ways through which data is gathered and then flows through the research process?

As Sasha Costanza-Chock (2019) advises, we might begin by looking at the work that is already being done by communities to gather, share, and disseminate knowledge—such as the series of Creative Resistance Workshops initiated by one of us (Roopa) in 2020, which model a values-based approach to collaborative research. Stemming from a profound personal discomfort with the reliance of her tech-based art practice on the power structures and protocols of Big Tech and its attendant logics, Roopa began bringing her fellow artists together in small groups to discuss the complicities, fears, and anxieties—along with hopes and desires—of working with emerging technology. The sessions revolved around seven prompts

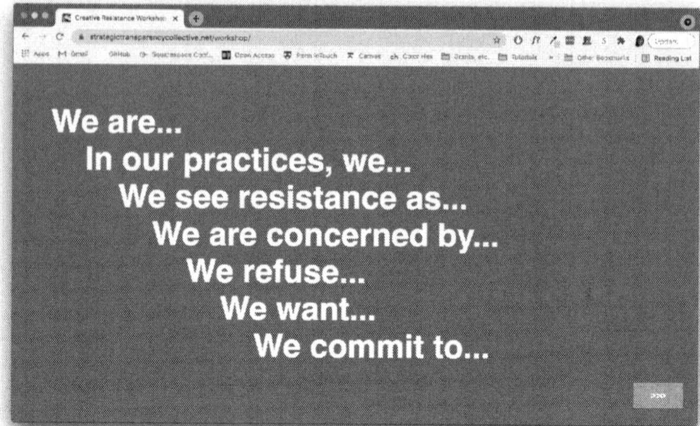


[Figure 6.1]. Screenshot of the Creative Resistance Workshop prompts. Courtesy Roopa Vasudevan.

for guided writing and discussion exercises and ended with the group writing a collaborative manifesto.

The process here counters the standard notion of participatory research. Rather than an external researcher parachuting into the community to be studied, the process was begun by a new media artist, attuned to the concerns facing her community. Instead of using a carefully guarded trove of research methods, the materials for the workshop are open source and available for anyone to use and adapt. Contrary to the traditional model of participation as validating the researcher's hypothesis, the workshops represent true collaborative knowledge building: There are no preconceived ideas about what the outcomes should be, letting ideas emerge organically from group activity. Roopa's approach adheres to what anthropologist John L. Jackson Jr. (2004) describes as a more vulnerable approach to reflexivity in research. Matching the vulnerability of her participants, she involves herself fully in each workshop, acknowledging that the questions she asks deeply affect her too.

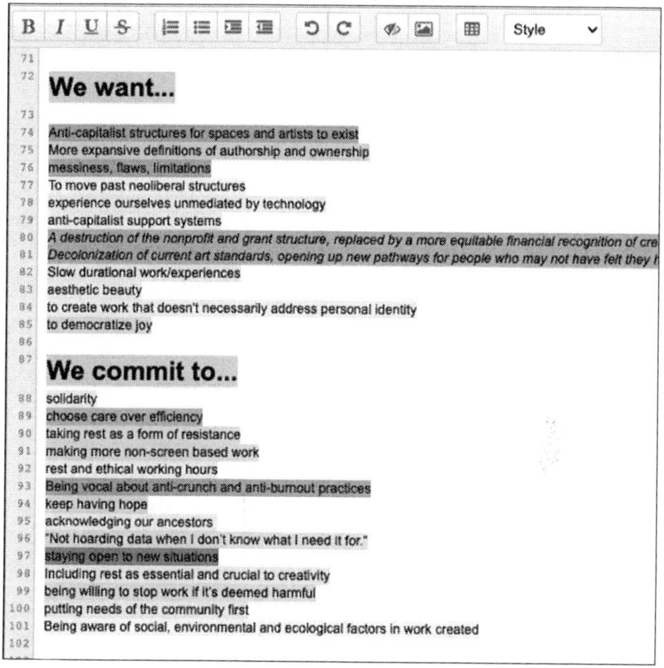

B I U S Style

## We want...

Anti-capitalist structures for spaces and artists to exist
More expansive definitions of authorship and ownership
messiness, flaws, limitations
To move past neoliberal structures
experience ourselves unmediated by technology
anti-capitalist support systems
*A destruction of the nonprofit and grant structure, replaced by a more equitable financial recognition of cre*
*Decolonization of current art standards, opening up new pathways for people who may not have felt they h*
Slow durational work/experiences
aesthetic beauty
to create work that doesn't necessarily address personal identity
to democratize joy

## We commit to...

solidarity
choose care over efficiency
taking rest as a form of resistance
making more non-screen based work
rest and ethical working hours
Being vocal about anti-crunch and anti-burnout practices
keep having hope
acknowledging our ancestors
"Not hoarding data when I don't know what I need it for."
staying open to new situations
Including rest as essential and crucial to creativity
being willing to stop work if it's deemed harmful
putting needs of the community first
Being aware of social, environmental and ecological factors in work created

[Figure 6.2]. A screenshot of a draft manifesto from the September 29, 2020, Creative Resistance Workshop. Courtesy Roopa Vasudevan.

The Creative Resistance Workshops are also spaces in which collaborators contribute to the final output and maintain sustained conversations. Roopa is also using the workshops as a launchpad for a larger platform—the Strategic Transparency Network—that, in just four years, has produced a public art project, an exhibition, an online and print publication, and the launch of an independent press imprint.

The framing of this platform as produced by a "network," rather than a single individual, is extremely important.[4] While it was initiated by a single person, the refusal to tie the work permanently to any single name opens the door to collective authorship.

[Figure 6.3]. Install view of We Refuse, We Want, We Commit, a Strategic Transparency Network exhibition at 292 Gallery (New York), March 2023. Photo by Daniel Johnson.

[Figure 6.4]. Wheatpaste poster installed as part of Take What You Can't Get at ABC No Rio (New York), November 2020. Courtesy of Roopa Vasudevan.

The invitation to a Creative Resistance Workshop is an invitation to make yourself comfortable, stay a while, and maybe even rearrange the furniture.

For a data fluencies praxis—expanded upon in the coda to this book—it matters how we collaborate. It matters how we work with each other and with varied communities through reciprocity, not extraction. Co-learning, co-research, and co-creation are key tactics that foster this approach. As the Facebook research example illustrates, digital information pathways are often taken for granted, allowing people to be taken advantage of through so-called terms of service. This is not a bug in the system—this is how these platforms have been designed. This example, and others like it, are the antithesis of our approach; they harness the appearance of "participation" as a mechanism for manipulating and maintaining market demand.

Markus Miessen (2016) advises that participation is a critical act of engagement: one that must be centered not only in the processes of a project but in the very premise of the work itself. A data fluencies approach disrupts the extractive processes of the status quo by working with people from the start to co-find problems, co-define possibilities, and co-create alternatives for both understanding and intervening in the systems that be. Engaging in this praxis can of course have an array of benefits for researchers, but the focus is primarily on the communities with whom we collaborate. If they don't benefit, there is no purpose in engaging in the work.

## Everyone Researches and Designs

As we have seen, knowledge is often conceptualized as emerging from an established hierarchy, where "expert" researchers recruit "participants" in order to test out hypotheses that they have already devised. Inviting people to "participate" in processes like this—or simply including them without consent, as illustrated by the Facebook study—often results in data that is extractive and nonreciprocal, where community members offer insight into their lives without receiving anything in return. This work then is used to elevate the careers of individual researchers, who could not have arrived at their results without the labor of the people they exploit.

But as scholars like Patricia Hill Collins (2008) and Sara Ahmed (2017) have argued, theory and knowledge flow from everyday life, not only from the academy. Everyone is a researcher in their own way; everyone is an expert of their own lived experience. We all can produce thoughts, generate ideas, and shift paradigms. Often it's simply a matter of who is taken seriously and who is not.

But it's not simply about expanding what counts as research and who counts as researchers. As Roopa's example shows, it's also about realizing that everyone creates. To return to a theme introduced in the first chapter, we believe these creative undercurrents can draw together diverse cultures into civilly engaged societies. Similarly, designer-researchers Henric Benesch and Onkar Kular (2020) posit that design is a prerequisite for an informed citizenship that can foster and claim more sustainable ways of living. In this way, all human beings are designers and researchers. We are activated as a collective to speak on issues that concern and affect us, moving us toward becoming co-producers and co-creators of knowledge.

## Co-Creating

What does co-creation look like? To start answering this question, we turn to the Night School for Data Fluencies to illustrate how frameworks for public engagement, co-creation, and co-design can foster renewed and multivocal perspectives on our data futures. As you'll see, it resonates with the Reclaim Project and Camp Kiki, discussed earlier in chapters 3 and 4.

### THE NIGHT SCHOOL

The Night School, developed by the Imaginative Methods Lab (IML) in the School of Interactive Arts and Technology at Simon Fraser

University, is a free, temporary school based in Vancouver, British Columbia. Guided by design fellow Samein Shamsher and Gillian, the project unfolds in various community centers, artist-run centers, and public libraries. It creates opportunities for community members to imagine different data futures while developing technical knowledge and skills. By 2025, more than three hundred people—including designers, artists, lawyers, teachers, philosophers, communication experts, writers, architects, youths, parents, grandparents, and a cyborg—have participated.

The school has experimented with diverse co-creation forms, drawn from futures-oriented design, including board games, performative role-play workshops, experimental walks, and storymaking sessions. Each creates different modes of participation: Some enable collective imagining; others support in-depth co-creation of objects or stories. Taken as a whole, they bring together the multivocal experiences and perspectives of communities from diverse geographical, cultural, and generational backgrounds.

To offer an example, one satellite engagement in Bilbao (ES) invited an international group of twenty undergraduate and graduate students, professors, and community members to play Fables for Imagining, a storymaking game that was designed by the IML in collaboration with Craig Badke. Drawing on the work of Daniela Rosner (2018), Saidiya Hartman (2021), and Donna Haraway (2019), the project employs fabulation as a meaning-making activity that uses the familiar tropes of storytelling through fables to create unfamiliar tales and to build a critical awareness of the world. The game helps participants co-create stories about the difficult yet important relationships they have with the digital platforms around them.

To begin, we shared what social media platforms we use. Spurred on by prompts, we told stories of our digital encounters. This process empowered each member of the group to be “experts of their experience” while playing a central role in knowledge production, idea generation, and concept development (Sanders and Stappers 2014, 24).

Through our research, we have found that simply asking people to write fables about their technological encounters leads to paralysis, as with the Camp Kiki participants when they first engaged with LARPing. The game, therefore, experiments with various prompting artifacts and activities to create a structured flow: Participants analyzed the antagonists and protagonists (human and nonhuman) of the social media platforms they were discussing; imagined the representative archetypes and multiple story arcs of these systems; purposely misread historic fables; and then wrote their own tales. Each co-created fable was then brought back to the IML to be edited, illustrated, and archived with the other fables collected over the course of the project's lifespan. The final versions will be shared with all participants in digital book form with a short essay contextualizing the project.

The fables, written in Bilbao, draw together a range of situated experiences and perspectives, addressing topics such as internet rabbit holes, tech accessibility, and social relationships developed online. They raise questions about power, values, and the structural inequalities that shape social media platforms in meaningful ways. For instance, three participants, Zainab Marvi, Karma Dabaghi, and P1, crafted a story about an experience one of them had with online schooling during the Covid-19 pandemic, using the figures of a monkey and a dragon (Figure 6.5).

### Monkey and the Dragon (A Zoom Story)

In a lush and vibrant land, lived two young friends—Monkey and Dragon. Monkey was clever and agile, moving seamlessly under the forest canopy. Dragon, with shimmering scales and powerful wings, soared above the clouds. Though different, they were inseparable at school, sharing dreams and laughter under the same roof.

When a mysterious pandemic swept the land, schools moved to the sky—accessible through a magic called the internet. Dragon adapted quickly, flying well above the treetops to find

[Figure 6.5]. *The Monkey and the Dragon: A Zoom Story,* illustration by Doan Truong, 2023.

strong signals. Monkey, however, struggled. The dense forest blocked the waves of magic, so he had to climb tall trees and mountains to gain access, growing more tired with every visit.

At first Dragon tried to help Monkey, sharing notes and encouragement. But as time passed, Dragon's view of the world shifted. The sky, vast and filled with opportunity, seemed open to all who dared to fly.

"Monkey, just climb higher," Dragon would say.

"I can't," Monkey would say, "My arms can't carry me that far."

Over time, Dragon stopped descending, lost in the endless horizon. Monkey, left behind, still dreamed of the sky but remained bound by barriers unseen from above. Their friendship faded, a bittersweet memory of a time when they stood on the same ground.

A second fable, written by Franca Lopez Barbera, Elise Talgorn, Heloisa Oliveira, and Andrés Amaya, painted the picture of the mental gymnastics required when engaging the push and pull of Instagram.

### The Rabbit and the Earthworm (An Instagram Story)

"Follow me! Do you want to see another cute kitten video?" said Rabbit while jumping enthusiastically from hole to hole.

Life for Rabbit was jolly and merry. He loved to discover new and exciting burrows to jump through. But with every new discovery, Rabbit's warren grew bigger and bigger.

"Up! Kardashian hole!"

"Left, Trump hole!"

"Down, Rihanna pregnancy hole!"

"Right, antivaxxers hole!"

Soon Rabbit grew tired. "Why so many holes?" he thought.

Known by all as both curious and friendly, Rabbit turned cynical and angry. It was just too much. So, Rabbit decided to take a break and stop jumping.

One day Earthworm popped his head into Rabbit's burrow where Rabbit was resting.

"Rabbit, why don't you jump anymore?" asked Earthworm. "I've been digging all over for you, but you are not following."

"Oh!" said Rabbit. "I'm exhausted!"

"I had no idea!" replied Worm.

[Figure 6.6]. *The Rabbit and the Worm: An Instagram Story,* illustration by Doan Truong, 2023.

> That very moment, Rabbit and Worm decided to make a pact: From there on in, Rabbit's burrow would have only two holes. And since then, Rabbit jumps from Kim Kardashian to kitten videos for all eternity.

More than simply tales of moral inquiry and caution, these fables built surprising solidarities, like those described in chapter 1, in two ways: one, others in workshops located across the world wrote similar stories; two, others reading the story found it echoed with their own experiences. Both the process and the fables thus foster a collective imagination and sensibility for our future selves and society, while extending the rights to research into the public domain.

As this chapter makes clear, co-creation is flexible yet structured, temporary yet lasting, imaginative yet material. It re-acts and counters; it creates surprising solidarities as it plays out of place. The Creative Resistance Workshops and Night School for Data Fluencies employ a "co-shaping" approach that transforms participation. Here, emerging knowledges and actions flow together. These co-creation projects not only reimagine how we collaborate and who counts in this process, but also construct parallel realities and alternate presents and futures that foster our fluencies.

## Notes

1 In 2018, former Cambridge Analytica employee Christopher Wylie revealed that the consulting firm had used data that had been harvested from millions of Facebook users—without their consent—for political advertising in the 2016 US presidential election. Cambridge Analytica purchased the data from an outside researcher, who Facebook claimed was collecting it for academic scholarship (Rosenberg et al. 2018).

2 Former Facebook employee Frances Haugen leaked thousands of internal company documents to the *Wall Street Journal* in 2021. Among them were documents showing that as early as 2020, Instagram researchers had presented work outlining the platform's detrimental effects on teenagers to leadership, but Facebook publicly downplayed these harms until the leak and its contents were reported (Wells et al. 2021).

3 Later reporting by Kashmir Hill (2014) found that language around "research" for academic purposes did not exist in the Facebook terms of service at the time of the study.

4 On several occasions, projects have been billed as produced by "members of the Strategic Transparency Network" rather than being authored by a sole artist.

## References

Ahmed, Sara. 2017. *Living a Feminist Life*. Duke University Press.

Benesch, Henric, and Onkar Kular. 2020. "The Right to Design." https://parsejournal.com/article/the-right-to-design/

Carberry, John. 2014. "Media Statement on Cornell University's Role in Facebook 'Emotional Contagion' Research." June 30, https://web.archive.org/web/20140703115856/http://mediarelations.cornell.edu/2014/06/30/media-statement-on-cornell-universitys-role-in-facebook-emotional-contagion-research/.

Collins, Patricia Hill. 2008. *Black Feminist Thought: Knowledge, Consciousness, and the Politics of Empowerment.* Routledge.

Confessore, Nicholas. 2018. "Cambridge Analytica and Facebook: The Scandal and the Fallout So Far." *New York Times,* April 4. https://www.nytimes.com/2018/04/04/us/politics/cambridge-analytica-scandal-fallout.html.

Costanza-Chock, Sasha. 2019. *Design Justice: Community-Led Practices to Build the World We Need.* MIT Press.

Dwoskin, Elizabeth. 2021. "Facebook Is Changing Its Name to Meta as It Focuses on the Virtual World." *Washington Post,* October 8. https://www.washingtonpost.com/technology/2021/10/28/facebook-meta-name-change/.

"Editorial Expression of Concern: Experimental Evidence of Massivescale Emotional Contagion Through Social Networks." 2014. *Proceedings of the National Academy of Sciences* 111 (29): 10779. https://doi.org/10.1073/pnas.1412469111.

Flick, Catherine. 2016. "Informed Consent and the Facebook Emotional Manipulation Study." *Research Ethics* 12 (1): 14–28. https://doi.org/10.1177/1747016115599568.

Haraway, Donna. 2019. "It Matters What Stories Tell Stories; It Matters Whose Stories Tell Stories." *A/B Auto/Biography Studies* 34 (3): 565–75. https://doi.org/10.1080/08989575.2019.1664163.

Hartman, Saidiya. 2021. "Intimate History, Radical Narrative." *The Journal of African American History* 106 (1): 127–35. https://doi.org/10.1086/712019.

Hill, Kashmir. 2014. "Facebook Doesn't Understand the Fuss About Its Emotion Manipulation Study." *Forbes,* June 29. https://www.forbes.com/sites/kashmirhill/2014/06/29/facebook-doesnt-understand-the-fuss-about-its-emotion-manipulation-study/.

Jackson, John L., Jr. 2004. "An Ethnographic Filmflam: Giving Gifts, Doing Research, and Videotaping the Native Subject/Object." *American Anthropologist* 106 (1): 32–42. https://doi.org/10.1525/aa.2004.106.1.32.

Kramer, Adam D. I., Jamie E. Guillory, and Jeffrey T. Hancock. 2014. "Experimental Evidence of Massive-Scale Emotional Contagion Through Social Networks." *Proceedings of the National Academy of Sciences* 111 (24): 8788–90. https://doi.org/10.1073/pnas.1320040111.

Meyer, Robinson. 2014. "Everything We Know About Facebook's Secret Mood-Manipulation Experiment." *The Atlantic,* June 28. https://www.theatlantic.com/technology/archive/2014/06/everything-we-know-about-facebooks-secret-mood-manipulation-experiment/373648/.

Miessen, Markus. 2016. *Crossbenching: Toward a Participation as Critical Spatial Practice.* Sternberg Press.

Rosenberg, Michael, Nicholas Confessore, and Carole Cadwalladr, Carole. 2018. "How Trump Consultants Exploited the Facebook Data of Millions." *New York Times,* March 17. https://www.nytimes.com/2018/03/17/us/politics/cambridge-analytica-trump-campaign.html.

Rosner, Daniela K. 2018. *Critical Fabulations: Reworking the Methods and Margins of Design.* MIT Press.

Sanders, Elizabeth B., and Pieter Jan Stappers. 2012. *Convivial Toolbox: Generative Research for the Front End of Design.* Bis.

Wells, Georgia, Jeff Horwitz, and Deepa Seetharaman. 2021. "Facebook Knows Instagram Is Toxic for Teen Girls, Company Documents Show." *Wall Street Journal,* September 14. https://www.wsj.com/articles/facebook-knows-instagram-is-toxic-for-teen-girls-company-documents-show-11631620739.

# Conclusion

Since we wrote the first draft of this book, the world has frayed even further. Everywhere we look, there are more and more obstacles to creating the futures—and the present—we want. But this has clarified for us how needed our projects, and others inspired by data fluencies, really are. In these pages, we have laid the foundations for data fluencies to continue to flourish, grow, and develop. As we have shown, data fluencies express emergent possibilities. To answer our questions about creating multivocal data fluencies and solidarities, data-fluent approaches bring forth more vibrant and just futures, pushing back waves of online hate, algorithmic manipulation, widespread surveillance, disciplining gamification, and the enclosure and privatization of public knowledge, research, and hope. Every chapter is a starting point, to push back against the algorithm, to counter the spread of hate, to re-imagine and re-act, to co-create instead of extract.

Currents of solidarities, re-action, countering, play, and co-creation run through our collaborations and approaches. While this book turns to specific projects to illustrate each core theme, the concerns of these projects overflow these chapter divides. The Reclaim Project counters toxic masculinity but also embraces co-creation in its student-led media productions. Camp Kiki celebrates play but also counters a rewards-based model of pedagogy. The Night School harnesses imagination for co-creation while also building robust solidarities. Thus, the projects under the Data Fluencies umbrella emerge from their places—from their contexts—but they also connect.

 Through the examples of our projects, we have argued that our future (and our present) is in peril, but that we can find opportunities to build the world we want with our communities. We have been active in developing data fluencies alongside communities from the very beginning. We reject the illusion of networked connections that can leave us anxious, overwhelmed, doomscrolling, and alone. Critical race, feminist, and queer frameworks of community remind us that we can foster social inclusion and meaningful solidarities. We do not have to exist in isolation—in fact, our well-being depends on one another and our connection to place.

Together, we have also pushed back on the idea of scalability. The world is a big place, and it can be easy to fall into the trap of thinking that the only things that matter impact everything, everywhere, all at once. Think back to the introduction, where we discussed the importance of dialects in fluency—how individuals and smaller groups make meaning through local inflections, accents, and slang—and how we can still communicate without needing to reach every corner of the world. As we have shown, in the world of data fluencies, gaps become interstitial spaces of possibility.

## Projects Out of Place

In this conclusion, we want to acknowledge some of the other projects from the Data Fluencies network that have been echoing through these pages.

Giulio Dalla Riva's team at the Otautahi Data Centre in Christchurch (Aotearoa New Zealand) has worked with a Data Activist in Residence, Mazharuddin Syed Ahmed, to produce a web interface for a large collection of reports, inquiries, policies, and public event records addressing the 2019 terrorist attacks in Christchurch. Leveraging LLM technology for community needs, they produced summaries of the texts that made analysis of the large dataset widely available to community members and researchers. Ahmed iteratively collaborated with community members in the Al Nor

Mosque to refine and shape the project. Two other Data Activists in Residence, Bianca Beebe and Byron Clark, also worked with Giulio's team. Bianca monitored and improved working rights for sex workers in New Zealand and produced a "cybersafety for activists" zine for social activists; and Byron developed an automated text analytical tool for podcasts in order to monitor white supremacist and far-right activity.

Ganaele Langlois and her team at York University in Toronto (Canada) along with Matt Canute at SFU have been developing speculative digital research methods that move away from surveillance, extraction, and capture—expanding the boundaries and techniques used within information studies. These methods incorporate performance, fiction, and digital art to rethink the concepts of the "persona" and sentiment. Through workshops delivered in Vancouver, New York, and Philadelphia, participants engaged with the Image and Affect tool, Agnostic Scraper, and the Authenticity and Conflict Analyzers. Designed to connect participants with the tools they need to better understand their datafied world, the workshops are also iterative, providing feedback that allows Langlois and her team to further refine their tools to be more accessible, equitable, and intuitive to use.

The Experimental Algorithmic Futures Working Group (EAFWG), initially co-led by Stephanie Dick and then co-led by Pippa, in addition to the Sentiment Analysis work detailed in chapter 2, has supported a varied collection of projects.

For example, Maureen Johnson León leads a collaborative project on ventilation as a social justice issue. In this project, an interdisciplinary team of researchers explores the paradigm of *clean air* from multiple analytical perspectives. Rather than leading from data science, Johnson León's team prioritizes historical and humanistic perspectives for looking at how ventilation in the built environment is entangled with labor justice, racial segregation, and policy directives. The team, including Stephanie Dick, Elaine LaFay, Kimberly Bain, Oriana Walker, Jiaqi Wen, and Adjua Akinwumi, is closely examining scientific sensibilities in the choices around measurement, modeling, and optimization, for indoor air quality and health, with special attention to how this type of analysis can inform knowledge around the complexity of novel threats such as pandemics and climate change.

Other projects in the EAFWG explore Indigenous knowledges, including Karrmen Crey's working group on Indigenous Epistemologies, and Caroline Running Wolf's FLAIR project, which works with Indigenous communities to train an ethical, multilingual voice AI designed to support language maintenance and reclamation. Pippa is also collaborating with Running Wolf, Cheyenne La Vallee, and Daniel Kennedy on a project examining the translation of principles of Indigenous Data Sovereignty into real-world projects in order to create a toolkit to help guide Indigenous communities to enact their sovereignty over their language data and much more.

As part of the Data Fluencies project, the Social Sciences Research Council (SSRC) has run a series of research development workshops. The first, in 2023, was organized on the theme of "Labor and Technology" in Vancouver (Canada); the second, in 2024, tackled the theme of "Drilling Down to the Data: Navigating Data Politics at the Heart of AI Policy" in Brooklyn (USA). The SSRC has also funded ten Dissertation Grants to a multivocal group of scholars working on projects dealing with data, technology, information, and social justice research, promoting the Data Fluencies' pursuit of more just and equitable futures through the responsible use of data and technology.

Carina Albrecht has led the group's Mellon fellows and the development of open-source courses in data fluencies that can be used, adapted, and retaught in other places, institutions, and contexts. Fred Lesage planned and taught the first of many summer programs we're calling the School of Data Fluencies for graduate students and other researchers, in the summer of 2025. We have also supported the work of two Data Fluencies Faculty Fellows, Susan Erikson and Victoria E. Thomas.

Roopa coordinated a series of three exhibitions in Boston (USA), Lexington (USA), and Vancouver (Canada). These exhibitions featured the work of six contemporary artists engaging with data and technology, as well as the community-engaged work led by other Data Fluencies researchers. Modeling a co-creative approach to exhibition planning, the galleries became sites of conversation between groups that do not typically share space—a chance to develop solidarities across difference.

Ioana Jucan led the Data Fluencies Theatre Project at Emerson College in Boston, *(Machine) Learning to Be,* built on her devised performance *Left and Right, or Being Who/Where You Are.* Jucan's interdisciplinary team presented co-created, participatory, devised, hybrid multimedia performances in Boston (USA) and Vancouver (Canada) that engage with algorithmic and AI systems.

Crucially, there's more to come.

Launched in 2025, Data Fluencies 2.0 will create sustainable models for humanities-centered multivocal AI projects, narratives, futures, and curricula. These emerging projects are a natural progression from the projects detailed in these pages, built on the methods, structures, and collaborations needed to effectively communicate in our data-filled world. Working across disciplines and institutions, Data Fluencies 2.0 will shape the emerging field of humanities and AI by showing how humanities knowledge and social justice are not things to be "added" to AI systems but essential for understanding their structure, content, impacts, and potentials. Not just understanding but also reimagining narratives generated about and through AI concerning the future of work and AI itself through technical, community-engaged, creative, futures-oriented, and historical projects that reject the premise that AI will render humans obsolete. These projects will also transform where and how AI is taught and researched at our institutions and beyond through humanities-based centers, courses, and workshops.

And there is also more to come from you, readers, as you take what we've offered in these pages and apply it to your own work, studies, teaching, and activism. We hope that you embrace the ideas that with data fluencies that seep through, reroute, and change the world around them, you can apply these principles to flow and adapt around the obstacles you identify. Even dams can open, rivers can create new paths, the slowest persistent drops of water can cut and reshape stone.

Taken as a whole, these projects reveal that although technologies are changing our world, we are not helpless bystanders or victims. Again, these are starting points for devising more ways to think, act, and imagine—to sense the worlds that could have been, might have been, and still are.

# Coda

## A Data Fluencies Praxis

So, what now? Where do we go from here?

We recognize the imaginative power of building capacities with communities. We don't want to operate with a deficit model always ruminating about the worst that can and might happen. As our Black and Indigenous comrades remind us, the worst *has* happened, and our power lies in keeping our humanity and creativity intact.

A data fluencies praxis is an *organic entity built collaboratively with each other and with varied communities* through reciprocity, not extraction. Co-learning and co-research are key tactics that foster this approach. As the Facebook research example in chapter 6 illustrates, digital information pathways are often taken for granted, allowing people to be taken advantage of through so-called terms of service. This is not a bug in the system—this is how these platforms have been designed. This example and others like it are the antithesis of our approach; they harness the appearance of "participation" as a mechanism for manipulating and maintaining market demand.

Engaging in this praxis can have an array of benefits for researchers, but the focus is more on the communities with whom we collaborate. If they don't benefit, there is no purpose in engaging in the work. Our research does not ever have to be scaled up—in fact, on many occasions it might be impossible to scale, as "community" is not a monolithic designation and different people have different needs.

While we also recognize that traditional approaches to disseminate scholarship are through academic publishing, this is not the only avenue of spreading and sharing knowledge. The Data Fluencies network has adopted a multimodal approach, informing the praxis that emerges from our work. We continue to engage an academic audience in traditional ways and publish scholarship in traditional outlets. This book is one such example, as is an upcoming publication by Gillian, Tara, and Kishonna entitled "Racial Harms and Digital Gaming." But, as chapter 6 reminds us, we also understand that academic publishing is not the only space in which new knowledge can be found. For example, Roopa is introducing our work to artistic audiences through a series of exhibits across the continent. Tara and team are activating collegiate audiences to be more than just passive bystanders in addressing manosphere cultures, by using social media to intervene in the pathways that create them. These examples reflect different forms of public scholarship—but because they are all generated from the community, they also adhere to a praxis centered on data fluencies.

Our praxis propels us to build upon existing research and expand it into a community-centered approach. Previous research methods—such as action research, participatory design, feminist methodologies, critical discourse, and others—all incorporate the public in some way. Some incorporate communities up front, some in the middle, and some at the end through the dissemination of research. A data-fluent approach acknowledges that communities must be included at every stage of the process, and as often as necessary. This helps both reduce power differentials and empower communities, as researchers in their own rights, to influence processes that directly impact their lives.

## Challenges with a Data Fluencies Praxis

One of the most significant challenges we've experienced is countering existing narratives surrounding academic institutions. A 2019 Pew research study found that the US public trusts practitioners more than researchers; they feel that scientists lack accountability and transparency (Funk et al. 2019). The public associates scientific and academic research with some of the most troubling, racist, and misogynistic examples of ethical lapses in history: the Tuskegee Syphilis experiments,[1] NYC's Fen-Phen Youth Study,[2] and other egregious demonstrations of medical racism.

Even outside of health research, scholars have often used their institutional power to gain access to communities in voyeuristic ways. For example, sociologist Alice Goffman's *On the Run*[3] (2014) at best violates the tenets of qualitative research by disregarding key ethical imperatives and disrespecting the complex and intersectional lives of Black folks; at worst, the work situates a white woman as a narrative savior in the lives of Black youths (Bonilla-Silva 2017). Residential boarding schools in North America were developed to "civilize" or assimilate Indigenous children into white, western, and Christian ideologies; but as Indigenous communities and scholars have subsequently told us, these schools were also a part of the genocidal project for white empire building. Even the internment of Japanese citizens in the United States was rooted in so-called research, which justified atrocious policies that continue to impact their descendants (Hickman and Fukawa 2012; Chen and Yu 2005).

It's no wonder that there is a continued lack of trust between communities and researchers—and all these troubling efforts used data in foundational ways. This is a core reason why a data fluencies praxis requires and demands ample time with community members to develop relationships before research even begins. Put another way, we ask people directly what they need and what research would most benefit them and their communities—an approach that, for example, Kishonna's team found invaluable while working with Black, Latinx, and Appalachian communities in Kentucky.

And while we do want to counter the mistrust that the public has with the scientific research process, we also want to engage a new model. We want to illustrate how publicly engaged, collaborative research *should* look. Communities and people are not units of analyses; they are embedded into the core of design. This process fosters a transparent process of research engagement, and knowledge production and dissemination. By being intentional and purposeful from the outset, we can demonstrate the power that these interactive and iterative research models might have on transforming our futures.

In addition to the multimodal approaches to dissemination that we have already discussed, we are also able to meet our communities where they are. Kishonna recently started a series of TikTok videos designed to share current issues that impact youths in gaming with their parents. Operating similarly to a Q&A session, there was a series of questions generated by parents and answered by the youths themselves. This helped boost dialogue intergenerationally by offering a space where guardians and youths could connect, in a place where the youths already were. Other researchers within the Data Fluences network utilize memes, zines, YouTube, in-person workshops, camps, and other ways to share information with communities. There are also examples within our network where public scholarship is *not* appropriate, as some communities need their identities and experiences protected from the public view. It is only when working intimately with these communities that these kinds of discoveries are made and respected.

## Fluencies

The examples and ideas we've discussed through these pages point to possibilities for more just and diverse futures among a flood of online hate, algorithmic manipulation, widespread surveillance, disciplinary gamification, and the enclosure and privatization of public knowledge, research, and hope. Across many registers, data fluencies express emergent possibilities, imagine new presents and re vibrant and just futures. They build, and build up, communi- o resist the harms of the world.

The projects under the Data Fluencies umbrella thus emerge from their place—from their context—but they also give us permission to connect across fluid solidarities. We push back on the illusion of networked connections that sometimes leave us anxious, overwhelmed, doomscrolling, and alone. The swells of thought fostered here give us the opportunity to dispel the doubt that decades of oppressive action and divisiveness have fostered. We are active in our hope for better futures. 

Taken together, the approaches outlined in these chapters help us listen for the worlds that could have been, might have been, and still are. These starting points for more ways to think, act, and imagine as we flow and reshape the currents of our data-driven world must be taken up with actions.

It is our hope that this body of work represents the interstitial space of possibility.

## Notes

1 The Tuskegee Syphilis Study was carried out by the United States Public Health Service (the precursor to the CDC) to examine the impacts of untreated syphilis in Black men. Despite penicillin being publicly available to treat the disease by 1947, it was intentionally withheld from participants. The study was responsible in part for the development of standardized Institutional Review Boards, along with research ethics guidelines such as informed consent and respect for persons (Jones 2012).

2 In the 1990s, Black and Latinx youths in New York City were recruited to ingest the drug Fen-Phen to determine whether it was associated with increased aggressive behaviors. Although the drug was banned in 1997, the experiment continued for another year (Brown 2003).

3 *On the Run* is an ethnographic work about the lives of young Black men in West Philadelphia. While Goffman's "deep cover" approach is not novel, what raised issues of concern were the extent and ethics of her participation in the lives of the people she studied. While observing, she witnessed community members committing crimes, and at times may be complicit in said crimes. Due to a variety of inconsistencies in her account, Goffman was also accused of fabricating and embellishing her data and failing to follow sociological ethics guidelines (Campos 2015). Additionally, Black scholars and community members suggested her treatment of Black life reduced the complexities as she was not immersed enough to understand certain Black practices (Lubet 2015).

# References

Bonilla-Silva, Eduardo. 2017. "What We Were, What We Are, and What We Should Be: The Racial Problem of American Sociology." *Social Problems* 64 (2): 179–87.

Brown, Elaine. 2003. *The Condemnation of Little B: New Age Racism in America.* Beacon Press.

Campos, Paul F. 2015. "Alice Goffman's Implausible Ethnography." *The Chronicle of Higher Education,* August 21. https://www.chronicle.com/article/alice-goffmans-implausible-ethnography/.

Chen, Fu-jen, and Su-lin Yu. 2005. "Reclaiming the Southwest: A Traumatic Space in the Japanese American Internment Narrative." *Journal of the Southwest*: 551–70.

Funk, Cary, Meg Hefferon, Brian Kennedy, and Courtney Johnson. 2019. "Trust and Mistrust in Americans' Views of Scientific Experts." Pew Research Center.

Goffman, Alice. 2009. "On the Run: Wanted Men in a Philadelphia Ghetto." *American Sociological Review* 74 (3): 339–57.

Hickman, Pamela, and Masako Fukawa. 2012. *Righting Canada's Wrongs: Japanese Canadian Internment in the Second World War.* James Lorimer & Company.

Jones, James H. 2012. *Tuskegee's Truths: Rethinking the Tuskegee Syphilis Study.* UNC Press Books.

Lubet, Steven. 2015. "Ethics on the Run." *The New Rambler Review,* May: 15–34.

# Authors

**Philippa R. Adams** is postdoctoral fellow at the Digital Democracies Institute at Simon Fraser University. She is program manager of the Data Fluencies project and co-principal investigator of its Experimental Algorithmic Futures Working Group.

**Wendy Hui Kyong Chun** is Simon Fraser University's Canada 150 Research Chair in New Media, professor in the School of Communication, director of the Digital Democracies Institute, and principal investigator of the Data Fluencies project.

**Kishonna Gray** is professor, author, and gamer who leads the Intersectional Tech lab and workshops in the School of Information at the University of Michigan. She is author of *Intersectional Tech* and is coeditor of *Feminism in Play.*

**Tara McPherson** is HMH Foundation Endowed Professor of Cinema and Media Studies at the University of Southern California School of Cinematic Arts and director of the Sidney Harman Academy for Polymathic Study. For Data Fluencies, she is principal investigator of the Reclaim Project.

**Gillian Russell** is associate professor in Simon Fraser University's School of Interactive Arts and Technology and director of the Imaginative Methods Lab. For the Data Fluencies project, she is principal investigator of the Public Night School.

**Roopa Vasudevan** is assistant professor in the Department of Art at the University of Massachusetts Amherst, and the principal investigator on the Data Fluencies Exhibitions.